in PROCESS

KIM BOYCE

WITH KEN ABRAHAM

CHARIOT
FAMILY PUBLISHING

Chariot Family Publishing™ is an imprint of David C. Cook Publishing Co.
David C. Cook Publishing Co., Elgin, Illinois 60120
David C. Cook Publishing Co., Weston, Ontario
Nova Distribution Ltd., Newton Abbot, England

IN PROCESS: DEVOTIONS TO HELP YOU DEVELOP YOUR FAITH
© 1994 by Kim Boyce with Ken Abraham

Unless noted otherwise, all Scripture quotations are from the New American Standard Bible, © the Lockman Foundation 1960, 1962, 1963, 1968, 1971, 1972, 1973, 1975, 1977.

Verses marked (NIV) are from the Holy Bible, New International Version, © 1973, 1978, 1984, International Bible Society. Used by permission of Zondervan Bible Publishers.

Verses marked (KJV) are from the Holy Bible, King James Version.

All rights reserved. Except for brief excerpts for review purposes, no part of this book may be reproduced or used in any form without written permission from the publisher.
Cover designed by Foster Design
Photography by Carlos Vergara
First Printing, 1994
Printed in the United States of America
98 97 96 95 94   5 4 3 2 1

Library of Congress Cataloging-in-Publication Data
Boyce, Kim.
In process : devotions to help you develop your faith / Kim Boyce, Ken Abraham.
p.   cm.
ISBN 0-7814-0822-9
1. Teenagers—Prayer-books and devotions—English. [1. Prayer books and devotions. 2. Christian life.] I. Abraham, Ken. II. Title.
BV 4850.B64   1993
242'.63—dc20   93-32713
                                                   CIP
                                                   AC

Contents

INTRODUCTION

Charge!.. 5

CORRECTING BLURRED IMAGES

The Facts of Love.. 11
Some New Lines 15
No Casual Affair 18
Sour Dates 23
Condomania 27

FLASH PHOTO

Costly Victory 33
Pure as the Driven Slush 38
So You Want to Be a Disciple 43
Signs of a Christian 47
Where Is God in the Dark? 50
Jesus Is Everything to Me 54

Self-portrait

Unique or You're Not	59
Shirley's Secret	63
Where Did Daddy Go?	67
Just Be Yourself!	71
How to Be a Name-Dropper	75

Wide-angle Lens

God and Politics	81
Helping the Homeless	85
Hurting People	89
Rx for Boredom	94
World Changers	97
What's Good about the Good News?	101

Home Videos

Our Incredible Van	107
Leisurely Days and Lonesome Nights	112
Switched!	115
I've Fallen and . . .	119
Trust God and Be Flexible	122
Until Now	125

Developing Your Own Pictures

From Goo, to the Zoo, to You?	131
What You See Is What You Get	135
The Dream Robber	138
Guarding Your Dreams	141
Getting Where You Are Going	145
You Can Do It!	150

Conclusion

Complete Exposure	155

in PROCESS

Charge!

I had the perfect picture in the viewfinder of my camera, and I was getting everything in focus. I was just about to snap the photograph, when I noticed a tiny yellowish light in the corner of the frame. "Oh, no!" I said out loud. "The low battery indicator is on!"

I knew what that meant. Without adequate power in the batteries, the flash on my camera would not activate. I could go through all the motions of taking a beautiful photograph, but the end result would be a hazy, dark, wasted mess.

The same thing is true of our "spiritual batteries." If we don't keep them adequately charged, the power won't be there when we need it. We can go through all the right motions, press all the right buttons, pretend that we have life totally in focus. We can even go so far as to fool other people into believing that we've been getting some fantastic photographs on film. But if our batteries aren't charged, we'll have no light, and the end result will be nothing but blank, empty, darkness.

As a Christian music artist, I am acutely aware of the need to keep my own spiritual batteries charged. I may perform a song a certain way in concert, and the Spirit of God may move powerfully in our midst. The next night, I may be in another town several hundred miles away singing that same song again. How tempting it becomes to rely upon the tried and true and think, *Hey, that worked last night; I'll bet it will work again tonight!*

Is that wrong? Not necessarily. But if I don't keep my spiritual batteries charged, before long my spiritual resources will run dry. Oh, sure, I can still go through the motions; I can do a performance. I may even be able to do the songs and say all the right words well enough that nobody in the audience would suspect that my spiritual batteries are run down. But I'd know . . . and even more importantly, God would know.

I've discovered that if I am going to do effectively what the Lord has called me to do, I need to check my focus every day. I need to tap into His supernatural power on a daily basis and allow Him to recharge my spiritual batteries. The same is true for you.

How can we do that? The best way I know to recharge your batteries is to get out your Bible, dust it off if you have to, and read a little bit every day. Don't try to read the entire New Testament in an afternoon. Go slowly. Take the Scripture in small sections and really think about it. Allow the Lord to speak to your heart and mind as you mull over His Word and how it applies to your life today. Then spend some time in prayer—talk to God—every day. You don't have to speak Old English in order for God to understand you. He understands whatever language you speak; better still, He understands the language of your heart.

This book is meant to help you get started charging your heart, or to stay charged up if you've already begun developing your devotional life. Either way, it is not intended to be your sole source of spiritual energy. This is just a "quick charge," a surge for your spiritual battery.

Here's how it works: I suggest that you read one devotional each morning before you go to work or school. I know how rushed you are, but this won't take long. Honest. In each devotional, you'll find some Scripture to read, think about, or act upon, as well as some practical ways to put the spiritual principles to work in your life. It is really important that you take the time to look up the Scripture passages, and not just read all the great stories.

Want to try one? Okay, this is for one of those days when you don't have much time, but you need a charge in your spiritual batteries.

>Step One: Read I Thessalonians 5:16-18. Once you find I Thessalonians, it shouldn't take you long to read these three short verses.
>Step Two: Do what the verses say.
>1. Rejoice always (vs. 16).
>2. Pray without ceasing (vs. 17).
>3. In everything give thanks (vs. 18).
>Step Three: Rejoice in the fact that you are alive and that Jesus is alive in you. Pray for yourself and for others. Thank God for everything you can think of—food, a bed to sleep on, your car to get you to school or work, the sunshine (or rain), your eyes (even though they don't want to stay open), your teeth (that you barely had time to brush), your hair (okay, forget that one). But you've got the idea, right? Okay, get going! Be positive, and be specific.
>No matter how hectic this day is, you can still rejoice throughout the day, praising God for who He is, and thanking Him for what He has done for you.

See! Simple, huh? Of course, not all the devotionals in this book are that short . . . well, actually, none of them are. Still, it will be time well spent, and you will discover that when you get to know more of the Word of the Lord, not only will you have some of the tough issues of our day in focus, but you will also have the Lord's power on board to deal with them.

in PROCESS | *Correcting Blurred Images*

in PROCESS
The Facts of Love

I used to think I knew everything about love, but the longer I study the subject, the more I realize how little of the facts of love I really understand. I'm not talking about the sensual facts of love; we are all aware of the power of physical attraction. But on a deeper level than mere animal magnetism, what is this thing called love? How can you find it? How can you keep it once you've found it?

Have you ever tried to define love? It's tough! Of course, there are different kinds of love. Nowadays, we use the same term to describe everything from love of God, family, and country, to love of baseball and chili dogs. It's not unusual to hear a classmate say, "Oh, I love Chris Jones" and "I just love the new menu at McDonald's" in nearly the same breath, and with nearly the same emotional intensity.

Undoubtedly, the best description of love ever written was penned by the apostle Paul to the first-century church in Corinth.

> *Love is patient, love is kind, and is not jealous; love does not brag and is not arrogant, does not act unbecomingly; it does not seek its own, is not provoked, does not take into account a wrong suffered, does not rejoice in unrighteousness, but rejoices with the truth; bears all things, believes all things, hopes all things, endures all things. Love never fails. . . . (I Corinthians 13:4-8).*

In the ancient Greek language in which Paul wrote this letter, three separate words were used to express various types of love. One of these, *eros,* was frequently used for passionate, physical expressions of love. The word usually had sexual overtones. It is the root of our words erotic and erotica. Today, these words are often used to describe many warped practices that are being passed off as the epitome of love. Apparently, Paul didn't see love that way. In his incredible description of love in I Corinthians 13, not once did he use the term eros. In fact, this word for love is not used anywhere in the New Testament!

The second Greek word that can be translated as love is *phileo.* This word is in the Bible, and it usually means a sort of brotherly love or a deep friendship. We get the name for our city of Philadelphia, the "city of brotherly love," from this word. For an example of phileo love, read John 21:15-17.

But the word Paul used to describe love in I Corinthians 13 is *agape*. Agape is the highest form of love because it is a self-giving, rather than a self-seeking, love. This is the kind of love God has for us, and it is the kind of love He wants us to have for each other. Jesus gave us the ultimate example of agape love when He said:

> *Greater love has no one than this, that one lay down his life for his friends (John 15:13).*

Then He went out and did it! He laid down His life on the cross; it wasn't taken from Him as many modern interpretations of Jesus' life falsely imply. He gave His life willingly for you and for me. The Bible states explicitly:

> *But God demonstrates His own love toward us, in that while we were yet sinners, Christ died for us (Romans 5:8).*

The more I think about love, especially Christ's love for us, the more I am convinced that true love requires a total commitment. It takes more than mushy-gushy feelings to give up your life for another person. True love—whether it is for the Lord, your family, or a potential marriage partner—is not a matter of your emotions; it is a matter of the will.

For example, when Gary and I married, it wasn't just an emotional and physical commitment that we made to each other. It was an intellectual and spiritual commitment as well. In a sense, each of us said to the other, "You are the person with whom I want to spend the rest of my life. I've made up my mind. From now on, for as long as I live, I give myself to you, to the exclusion of all others. After God, you are my top priority."

Some people might say, "What? Are you kidding? That sort of commitment is just too radical; it's totally unrealistic. Nowadays, nobody commits to anybody for any length of time, without any strings attached, with no reservations. That's just not possible in this day and age!"

Maybe it's not possible, if you make that kind of promise based only upon your own personality, looks, money, or willpower. In your own strength, even with the best of intentions, that sort of commitment is difficult. After all, who knows what may happen in the future? How can you commit yourself for tomorrow when you can barely handle today?

But with Jesus Christ in the center of a relationship, unconditional love is not just possible, it is the norm. Scripture says:

> *Beloved, if God so loved us, we also ought to love one another (I John 4:11).*

For more about God's love for us and how we are to love others, read I John 4:10—5:3. As you look over these verses, pay extra close attention to how freely God expresses His love to you. The glaring difference between God's agape, unconditional love, and our selfish, "I'll love you as long as it is convenient," sort of love is clearly shown in this passage.

Selfish love says, "I'll love you if you meet a certain set of conditions or because of certain circumstances. But if those conditions or circumstances change, my love for you may change too."

God says, "I love you, period. No strings, no gimmicks, no hidden agendas. I love you."

This is where being a Christian makes so much sense to me. Jesus Christ has already proven His unconditional love for us. And—here is where it gets really exciting—Jesus offers to fill our lives with that same sort of love, His love, God's agape love.

Those facts of love will stand the test of time!

ZOOM IN

1. A line from the title song of my "Facts of Love" album, says, "Sometimes I wonder how I ever lived before You came my way." Have you ever felt that way, that without Jesus you couldn't make it? Today, thank Him for His overflowing love that gives you the strength to face each day with renewed hope.
2. What are some practical ways you can apply the truths of I John, chapter 4, to your walk with the Lord?
3. Isn't it interesting that John says in I John 4:12 that no one has seen God at any time. Then, right after that he says, "If we love one another, God abides in us, and His love is perfected in us." Why do you suppose John linked these two statements so closely together?

in PROCESS
Some New Lines

One of the great blessings of having a music ministry is the opportunity I have to meet and work with some incredible men and women Bible teachers. One such man who has left an indelible impression upon my life is Josh McDowell. Josh, as you may know, is a best-selling author and has been a traveling speaker for Campus Crusade for Christ for more than twenty years. Through his books, videos, and personal appearances, literally thousands of people have come to know Jesus.

A few years ago, Josh spearheaded a campaign called "Why Wait?" which, through education, encourages high school and college-age students to abstain from immoral sex. At the height of the campaign, I was privileged to be part of a series of concerts around the country which featured Josh, the band Petra, and myself. It was a great lineup and thousands of guys and girls responded positively to the message of Christ. Many Christian young men and women also committed themselves to maintaining (or regaining) their sexual purity.

Somewhere along the tour, Josh and Petra came up with one of the wildest, but most effective T-shirts I have ever seen. The idea for the shirt originated with a church youth group in Florida. The members had gotten fed up with constantly being on the defensive about their commitment to virginity and sexual purity. They had heard all the tired, worn-out lines that guys and girls used to pressure their dates into having sex before marriage, so they decided it was time to make up a few lines of their own. The youth group collected the sayings, printed them on some T-shirts, and started wearing them around town. That may not sound all that outrageous to you, but check out a few of the slogans they were wearing:

- I make my lifelong decisions with my head, not my hormones.
- I'm saving sex for marriage.
- It's just not worth it!
- Because I want a real honeymoon.
- Real men don't act like animals.
- It's a thrill that could kill.
- I don't owe it to anyone.
- AIDS is forever.
- I'm not weird; you're weird!
- I want real love, not a cheap substitute.
- You don't want me; you want it.
- I'm not ready for Junior yet.
- You should accept me for who I am, not for what I have to give you.
- I respect myself too much.
- Any boy can, but a man can wait.
- 33,000 Americans will get a sexually transmitted disease today. (This number has nearly doubled since the youth group first printed their shirts.)
- If you cared, you wouldn't dare.
- If you really loved me, you wouldn't ask.

Pretty powerful punches, huh? And a lot of good, common sense. Can you imagine wearing a T-shirt with one of those messages emblazoned on it?

Josh and Petra got permission from the youth group to print even more shirts, and the message continues to spread: The only safe sex is sex with your marriage partner. That's the only sex God blesses.

Two passages in Proverbs give some excellent advice about the dangers of sex outside of marriage. Read Proverbs 5:1-23 and Proverbs 7:6-27. Notice that both passages mention that the path of immorality leads to Sheol, which people in Old Testament times understood as a sort of netherworld, the place of the dead—hell.

ZOOM IN

1. Think of some of the ridiculous lines guys and girls use in their attempts to get what they want sexually. Have you ever been the target of someone pressuring you for sex? How did it make you feel?

2. Maybe you have already sinned in the area of your sexuality. Perhaps you never realized premarital sex was wrong, or you thought it was okay as long as you were in love. Or, maybe you knew what God has said concerning sex outside of marriage, but you went ahead anyway, with your conscience screaming like a siren. Regardless of how or why you committed sexual sin, you can be forgiven. You can be clean and know that as far as God is concerned, it is as though you never sinned in the first place. In other words, your "spiritual virginity" will be restored and you will once again be sexually pure.

How? Just ask Him! Confess the fact that you have sinned. God already knows, so don't worry about blowing your cover with Him. Remember His promise:

If we confess our sins, He is faithful and righteous to forgive us our sins and to cleanse us from all unrighteousness (I John 1:9).

Then ask the Lord for the moral strength to go and sin no more (John 8:11).

in PROCESS

No Casual Affair

Mary shuddered as she tried to think of an adequate way to break the news to her boyfriend, Joseph. She knew that she was a virgin, yet how could she ever explain to Joe what the angel of the Lord had told her in a dream? Still, she had to try.

"Um, Joe . . ."

"Yeah, Mary? What's up?"

"Er, ah, Joe, we need to talk."

"Sure. How about after work tonight? I should be done around 6:30. Why don't I meet you down at the deli?"

"Joseph. We need to talk now."

Joseph noticed the furrow creasing the forehead of his beautiful bride-to-be and realized that something serious was troubling her. "Mary," he said firmly, yet somehow tenderly, "what's wrong?"

Mary tugged at Joseph, pulling him toward the exit of the small carpenter's shop. Joseph instinctively followed her out the door, where they barely escaped the listening ears and watchful eyes of Joseph's boss.

"Joseph, I'm pregnant."

"You're what?" He recoiled in horror.

"I'm going to have a baby . . ."

"That's impossible! Why we've never even . . ." Joseph stopped in mid-sentence, his countenance turning suddenly livid. He knew that he had never had sex with Mary, but if she really was pregnant, that meant . . .

"Mary! How could you do this to me? I promised you that we would get married as soon as I could save enough money to get us a decent place to live . . . we announced our engagement at church . . . and now, you tell me that . . . oh, Mary! I don't believe this!"

Joseph paced back and forth on the dusty street, his hurt and anger blinding him to the passersby who were staring at him and Mary.

"Joseph," Mary said softly.

"What?" he responded harshly, and much more loudly than necessary.

"I didn't."

"You didn't what?"

"I didn't . . . you know . . . I didn't do anything with anyone. An angel appeared to me one night and scared me half to death. The angel told me that I was going to become a mother, and . . . well . . . I know this sounds a little crazy, but . . . the angel said that the Holy Spirit would come upon me and that I will give birth to the Son of God!"

"Yeah, sure. Right, Mary. And I'm Pharaoh the Great."

"It's true, Joseph! The angel said that God's power would come upon me and cause me to become pregnant."

"That's enough, Mary! I've had it. That is the last straw. It's bad enough that you have cheated on me, but then to blame this whole mess on God . . ."

Okay, so it probably didn't happen quite that way. But the people in the Bible were real people and had to deal with real-life problems just as you and I do. I'm sure it wasn't any easier for Mary and Joseph in that situation than it would be for one of your friends. Still, it's amazing the way they handled things. Check out the details in Matthew 1:18-25 and Luke 1:26-37.

Oh, yeah . . . the baby's name? Wonderful, Counselor, Immanuel, Jesus.

Have you ever wondered what the world would be like if Mary were alive and pregnant today, and some pro-abortion group got in touch with her? After all, by today's society's warped standards, Mary would have several compelling "reasons" why the only logical "solution" to her "problem" would be an abortion.

1. She was a teenager. Most Bible scholars believe that Mary was probably in her early teens when she became pregnant. That meant no formal education for Mary.

   It's hard to get anywhere nowadays without an education. Some schools are providing child care for teenage moms in a valiant but misguided effort to help. We'd all be better off if the schools would teach the truth: more than one million unmarried teens get pregnant every year, because they have bought the lie that says premarital sex is the best thing since the candy bar.

2. Mary was not married.

   Single parenting has never been easy, and still isn't. Talk to any single parent today and he or she will tell you it's tough being both Mom and Dad to a child. It is economically, emotionally, and physically draining. Maybe that's why God originally designed families to be made up of both parents.

3. She was economically poor.

   Many pregnant teens have no education, no husband, no job; all in all, a bleak picture. Many feel their only recourse is to hit the streets, taking any menial jobs that anyone offers, or perhaps worse, sinking into a life of prostitution.

4. Having a baby outside of marriage was extremely embarrassing and inconvenient.

   Though becoming more "acceptable" in today's society, unwed mothers are not looked upon most favorably. And especially in Mary's day, such situations were not regarded lightly by the community; nor with much compassion. The locals considered her a branded woman, used property. No man would want her for any purpose other than his own selfish gratification, and no "decent" woman would dare to be seen in her company.

For any one of these reasons, if alive today, Mary might be encouraged to have an abortion. Can't you hear the counselors trying to help her make up her mind?

"It's just a bunch of tissue, Mary. The fetus won't feel a thing."

"Mary, you are an intelligent young woman. Don't allow this little problem to inconvenience your life."

"You're young, Mary. You can have other children when you want to have them."

Whew! I'm sure glad Jesus had a smart mom.

ZOOM IN

1. Have you ever noticed that most people who favor abortion prefer to talk about the fetus (which is Latin for "unborn child"), rather than talk about a baby? Why do you think they make the distinction?
2. When someone says he or she is "pro-choice," don't be deceived. "Pro-choice" is actually pro-death, the death of a beautiful, unborn human baby.
3. A lot of rhetoric gets tossed around in the abortion debates. Today, begin to educate yourself about the real issues. Check out the facts, and you will quickly come to one inevitable conclusion: when a baby is purposely aborted, a life is purposely destroyed.
4. How should you respond when a friend or family member becomes pregnant outside of marriage?

    You could yell, scream, criticize, and condemn, but now is not the time for a lecture; now is a time for tender, loving care and understanding. The victim of a premarital pregnancy needs to know that God still loves and accepts her. She needs to know that you are not going to abandon or ostracize her. Certainly, you don't want to condone immorality. Jesus never trifled with sin; nor did He attempt to excuse it. He did, however, continue to love the sinner (John 8:1-11). You should do the same.

An unwed mother also needs a listening ear. Encourage her to talk about her feelings, fears, her future. Pray with her and encourage her to seek forgiveness and a fresh start with the Lord.

An unwed mother needs practical help too. Many churches and other organizations are now offering more than pro-life literature. They are putting their time, money, and love on the line and offering to provide food, shelter, clothing, and accurate information for girls faced with premarital pregnancy. Many ministries will also help once the baby is born, or they will help arrange for the child of an unwed mother to be adopted by a Christian family if the birth mother so decides.

One such Christ-centered source of information and help that I highly recommend is Mercy Ministries of America, founded by Nancy Alcorn. Mercy Ministries takes in pregnant girls from all walks of life, from all across America (free of charge), and offers them help and hope to begin rebuilding their lives on a solid foundation. For free information, write: Mercy Ministries of America, P.O. Box 150829, Nashville, TN 37215; or call 615-385-0496.

5. What if you or somebody close to you has already had an abortion? Remember, God has not given up on you. He still loves you in spite of your mistakes, failures, and sins. Although abortion is horrible, it is not the unpardonable sin. If you are willing to confess your sins to the Lord and ask Him to forgive you, He will do just that (I John 1:9).

You can start over, clean, fresh, forgiven. Jesus forgave the woman caught in the act of adultery, and gave her a new lease on life. He told her, "Neither do I condemn you; go your way. From now on sin no more" (John 8:11). If you are willing to turn away from your past sinful practices and sincerely ask Him to give you another chance, His message is the same to you.

in PROCESS
Sour Dates

In recent years, several highly publicized court cases focused attention on a crime that prior to this, few women, and even fewer men, wanted to admit existed—namely, date rape. It's an ugly subject, but one we must think about. In fact, we must do more than just think about it. We need to take positive, preventative steps to avoid ever being victimized or becoming the victimizer in a date-rape situation.

First, let's define terms. Rape occurs when a woman is sexually violated, when she is forced to have sex against her will. Many people think such a heinous crime is usually committed by a gang of thugs, like the gang who jumped a jogger in New York City's Central Park, and in a wild spree of unmitigated, uncalled-for aggression, beat and repeatedly raped the woman. Others hold on to Hollywood's warped portrayals of some psychopathic killer preying upon scantily clad young women who are minding their own business in their college sorority house. Both pictures of rape are distorted.

In fact, according to *Time* magazine (June 3, 1991, p. 48), "Most women who get raped are raped by people they already know—like the boy in biology class, or the guy in the office down the hall, or their friend's brother."

The Center for the Prevention and Control of Rape joined Mary P. Ross, Ph.D., in a three-year study of 6,100 undergraduate students on thirty-two college campuses across the U.S. Their study revealed some startling statistics:

In focus

- One in four of the young women surveyed was a victim of rape or attempted rape.
- Eighty-four percent of those raped knew their attackers.
- For both men and women, the average age when a rape incident occurred (either as perpetrator or victim) was eighteen and a half years old.
- Seventy-five percent of the men and fifty-five percent of the women involved in date rapes had been drinking or taking drugs just before the attack.

(Cited by Josh McDowell in *Research Almanac and Statistical Digest,* 1990, p. 95.)

Ironically, in a telephone poll conducted by Yankelovich Clancy Shulman for *Time* and CNN (the Cable News Network), 66 percent of the eighteen to thirty-four year olds surveyed did not believe a woman who is raped is partly to blame if she is under the influence of drugs or alcohol. Seventy percent of this group didn't believe it should matter whether or not she was dressed provocatively. Over 76 percent said she should not be blamed if she was raped after agreeing to go to a man's room or home (cited in *Time;* June 3, 1991, p. 51).

With all due respect to Yankelovich Clancy Shulman's findings, I think that is extremely idealistic. While it is never admissible for rape to occur, if you want to avoid date rape or any unwanted sexual advances, you are best off if you stay out of such compromising positions.

One of the most shocking stories in the Bible is an account of acquaintance rape. You can find the story in II Samuel 13:1-19. Let me warn you; it is not a pretty picture.

In this passage, Amnon, a son of King David, raped his half-sister Tamar. The Bible says that Amnon loved Tamar (vs. 1), but sadly, immediately after he had sex with her, he didn't want anything further to do with her. In fact, the Scripture poignantly states:

Then Amnon hated her with a very great hatred;

*for the hatred with which he hated her was
greater than the love with which he had loved her
. . . (vs. 15).*

Poor Tamar! She wasn't "asking for it," as some men allege when they are charged with rape. She wasn't dressed provocatively, either. She truly was an innocent victim. She had gone to a guy's apartment all by herself thinking she was there to help a sick man. She had no idea she was being set up. Amnon eventually paid for his crime with his own life, murdered at the command of his brother Absalom (13:28, 29). Tamar was devastated. Not only had she cruelly lost her virginity, but she also lost her brother over this sin.

ZOOM IN

What are some things we can do to avoid date rape? Here are some simple suggestions:

1. Be careful how you "flirt." Flirting used to be rather innocuous, a woman batting her eyelashes, or smiling at just the right time, or peeking her face out from behind a hand-held fan on a warm summer evening, or a guy raising his eyebrows Tom Selleck style. Nowadays, flirting is almost a forgotten art. It's meet, greet, and go for the goods.

   Nevertheless, flirting is part of the male-female equation that will never go away, no matter how sophisticated (or unsophisticated) the dating scene becomes. I'm not naïve enough to believe that you will never flirt with the opposite sex. Be careful, though. Don't advertise something you are not intending to make available. And don't make available anything you shouldn't!

2. Be careful how you dress. Christian men and women need to be aware that clothing makes a statement about their character. It is sheer nonsense to dress like a sleaze or a tease and then say, "But that's not who I really am. I'm not that kind of person." Oh, really? How

are people to tell?

I'm not saying we shouldn't keep our wardrobes up to date. I love to dress stylishly, and I believe God wants us to look good. As His children, our appearance is an outward reflection of what His Holy Spirit is doing within us. We can glorify God by our physical appearance. But let's not kid ourselves; it is also possible to give the impression that we are not considering Christ in our appearance.

3. Be careful of drugs and alcohol. Personally, I do not touch drugs and I'm a teetotaler when it comes to alcohol. That works for me, so I can heartily recommend you do the same. It is important that you don't do drugs or drink, but you also need to stay away from parties where drugs and alcohol are freely available. Keep in mind the high correlation between date rape, and drugs and alcohol.

Furthermore, if you are dating someone who is using the stuff, get out of that relationship as fast as you can!

4. Be careful where you go on your dates. Most couples want to spend time alone; usually the more serious the relationship, the more privacy a couple desires. That's understandable, but it is also dangerous. If you are spending a lot of time alone, you had better establish some strict guidelines concerning your physical expressions that don't violate your moral principles!

In the early stages of your dating relationship, it is smart to stay in a group and in a public place. Never go back to the home, apartment, or room of a person you are just getting to know. Frankly, until the relationship has progressed in the direction of marriage, you would be much safer staying out of those places, period.

5. Always remember, No means No! Regardless of the circumstances, when a young woman (or a young man) says "No," to any sexual involvement, that decision should be respected.

in PROCESS

Condomania

recently, a major cable television network aired an hour-long talk show: "What Every High School Student Needs to Know About Condoms." The panelists discussing the subject included several sexually active high school students who admitted on the air they were having sex with an assortment of partners. One segment of the show even considered how gays could "protect" themselves. All of the participants on the show expressed no hesitation at having sex, because, after all, they were being "responsible" by using condoms.

Only one high school-aged young woman stated a preference for sexual abstinence as the best way to protect herself against unwanted pregnancy and sexually transmitted diseases. Later, however, she undermined her own argument by saying, "I believe in sexual abstinence, but I always carry a condom or two in my purse, just in case." Apparently, her idea of sexual abstinence depended more upon opportunity than moral purity.

The "highlight" of the show was a skit in which performers, playing the part of high school students, demonstrated how to talk to your partner about using condoms. The audience and the talk show host applauded wildly. They responded as though the message conveyed by this skit was a lifesaver for this generation of young men and women. Condoms, they implied, are the cure-all for AIDS, herpes, and fear of pregnancy. Sadly, the show misled its audience in several vital areas.

Hardly a word was spoken advocating sexual abstinence before marriage and sexual faithfulness within marriage. When abstinence was mentioned at all, it was always in the context of how "impossible" it is for modern youth to maintain sexual purity, and how unreasonable it is for anyone to expect healthy high school students to control their sexual desires. The prevailing contention was: Kids are going to have sex no matter what, so we better teach them to use condoms so they can have "safe sex." One solution implied by the TV show was that high school students, male and female, should carry a condom at all times. What a joke! And what an insult to the intelligence and integrity of an entire generation!

On the first page of a brochure entitled "Condoms and Sexually Transmitted Diseases . . . Especially AIDS" (a 14-page pamphlet the U.S. government sends free of charge to anyone asking for the truth about condoms), the first paragraph following the introduction reads:

> The surest way to avoid these diseases (AIDS, chlamydia, genital herpes, genital warts, gonorrhea, hepatitis B, and syphilis) is not to have sex altogether (abstinence). Another way is to limit sex to one partner who also limits his or her sex in the same way (monogamy).

The government pamphlet goes on to say in the next line:

> Condoms are not 100 percent safe, but if used properly, will reduce the risk of sexually transmitted diseases, including AIDS.

Then in dark, bold type the brochure states:

> Protecting yourself against the AIDS virus is of special concern because this disease is fatal and has no cure.
>
> ("Condoms and Sexually Transmitted Diseases . . . Especially AIDS," Department of Health and Human Services Publications FDA 90-4239, 1993, p. 1.)

Isn't that interesting? The preceding information is not coming from some Bible-wielding, wild-eyed fanatic ranting and raving about the dangers of immoral sexual conduct, nor is it coming from your concerned youth leader who is trying to keep you from destroying your life by touting the advantages of abstinence. That message is coming straight from the people in the government agency whose job it is to know the truth about "safe sex." Incidentally, they are also the agency charged with the morbid task of keeping track of how many people have died of AIDS.

The government brochure points out the second fallacy of the TV show promoting the use of condoms. Simply stated: Abstinence works, condoms don't! Some experts estimate that condoms fail in fourteen out of every one hundred cases. Condoms are far from foolproof. They must be used properly, and they must be used every time a couple has sex. Otherwise, that couple is wide open to the possibility of pregnancy or sexually transmitted diseases.

In answer to the question, "Will a condom guarantee I won't get a sexually transmitted disease?" the government brochure again cautions:

> No. There's no absolute guarantee even when you use a condom. But most experts believe that the risk of getting AIDS and other sexually transmitted diseases can be greatly reduced if a condom is used properly. In other words, sex with condoms isn't totally "safe sex," but is "less risky" sex (Ibid., p. 4).

Less risky? If Gary and I were about to board a plane to a concert and the pilot told us his plane was "less risky" than some others, his words wouldn't exactly inspire confidence, especially if he said, "Yes, this plane only crashes fourteen out of every one hundred flights." I think we'd be taking the bus to that concert!

Do you really want less risky sex? Or, do you want the best sex life possible? Then decide today that you will have sex with only one person—your marriage partner! And pay close attention to what the apostle Paul says in I Corinthians 6:9-20.

ZOOM IN

1. Why do you suppose so many people in leadership positions in our nation refuse to admit that God has a better idea when it comes to our sexuality?
2. Why do you think there is such an emphasis upon "safe sex" or "less risky" sex, rather than as God's Word teaches, that sex should be saved until marriage and then kept within marriage?
3. Start today to become more aware of accurate information concerning condoms, AIDS, and other sexually transmitted diseases. Don't believe everything you see on TV about the subjects; many people seem to have their own agenda when it comes to disseminating truthful information about AIDS and other sexually transmitted diseases. I do too. My agenda is to tell you what the Bible says about your sexuality.

in PROCESS *Flash Photo*

in PROCESS

Costly Victory

Most Christians today confess some degree of confusion when discussing the blood of Jesus. They tend to regard "the blood" as a reference to some archaic ritual, left over from a less sophisticated society; a needless reminder of our gory past that retains little significance or relevance for today's positive, upbeat, upscale Christianity.

Perhaps part of our perplexity results from such puzzling biblical expressions as "drinking Christ's blood" or "washing our robes in the blood of the Lamb." What does that mean to anyone who was not raised in Sunday school? Even more confusing to many new Christians are some of the lyrics to the songs we sing in church:

> There is power in the blood!
> Are you washed in the blood of the Lamb?
> What can wash away my sins?
> Nothing but the blood of Jesus.

For many young believers, these songs seem almost absurd, making absolutely no sense at all. What does the blood have to do with high-tech media ministries? Where does the blood fit into our contemporary Christian music? What significance does the blood have in how I live my life? These are valid questions for a generation that Francis Schaeffer often described as having no "Christian memory."

In saying that, Schaeffer was referring to the fact that most of our parents had family members (or could remember family members) who were Christians, or at least lived by a moral code based upon Judeo-Christian ethics. Even nonbelievers could relate to many of the principles contained in the Ten Commandments (Exodus 20:3-17) and Jesus' Sermon on the Mount (Matthew 5:1—7:29).

In our society today, however, many of your friends and mine no longer have a "Christian memory." Their parents may not be Christians, and often, they don't have any other friends (besides you) or relatives who are genuine Christians. Since their values are not based upon God's Word, frequently our friends have little understanding about sin, its seriousness, or its consequences.

Fortunately for us, God's heart broke over the problem of our sinfulness long before ours did. He put together a plan in which His pure Son, Jesus Christ, could pay the price for your sins and mine with His blood, so we might be free of the death penalty we so readily deserve for our sins.

The apostle Paul attempted to explain this concept to the Philippians when he encouraged them to have the same

> *... attitude ... which was also in Christ Jesus, who, although He existed in the form of God, did not regard equality with God a thing to be grasped, but emptied Himself, taking the form of a bond-servant, and being made in the likeness of men. And being found in appearance as a man, He humbled Himself by becoming obedient to the point of death, even death on a cross (Philippians 2:5-8).*

The following story will show you what Paul means.

In the early 1950s, before the transplanting of human body organs became commonplace, a young boy developed a deadly kidney infection. Doctors worked around the clock in their attempt to save the young man, but all of their efforts were failing. The boy's kidneys were so diseased, they could not possibly purify his system. There seemed to be no hope; nothing could be done but to stand by helplessly and watch the boy die.

In desperation, one of the doctors suggested an idea to the dejected parents. "It's never been done before," he said hesitantly, "but if we can find a person whose blood type is the same as your son's, maybe . . . just maybe, we could run the blood of your boy through the system of the healthy person. Perhaps, if we proceeded slowly, taking just a little of the blood at a time, the kidneys of the healthy person could do the work that the boy's system cannot do."

"Let's try it!" the parents exclaimed almost simultaneously.

"You must understand. This has never been done before. We have no idea what will happen, and we cannot guarantee success. There is great risk involved here, for your son as well as the donor," warned the doctor.

The parents looked hopefully at each other and nodded. "It's our only chance, Doctor," the father answered. "Let's do it."

"All right, we must hurry. Does anyone here have the same blood type as the boy?"

"I do," said the dad.

"And you would be willing to volunteer?" the doctor asked, his concern evident in the tone of his voice.

"I will," responded the father.

"Do you understand the risks involved here?" the doctor implored.

"Yes, I do," the father answered soberly. "Let's get on with it."

Quickly the medical staff tested the father's blood to make certain it was the same type as the boy's. They prepped the father as if he were being operated on, wheeled his gurney into the operating room, parked it parallel to his son's, and went to work.

They tenuously arranged tubing from the father to the son and back again, so the dad's system could take upon itself the impurities of his son, cleansing the boy's blood and returning him to health. As the process began to take effect, instantly, the father's temperature shot up. At the same time, slowly, the boy's fever began to recede, and his temperature came down. After a while, both the father and the son were out of critical danger and the operation was hailed as a huge success.

Seven days later, the boy was perfectly well and was released from the hospital, along with his father, to go home. The family was reunited for only two days when the father's temperature suddenly skyrocketed, and almost immediately, he fell over dead.

The boy lived, but it cost the life of his dad. His father had taken upon himself the sickness, fever, disease, and death that rightfully had belonged to his child. Only one thing motivates a person to do something such as that—love.

Though it is incomprehensible to our finite minds, something similar happened at Calvary when Jesus took upon Himself our disease of sin. He who was absolutely pure took on our awful impurity. It cost Him His life, but as a result, we are able to live. The apostle Paul summed it up when he wrote:

> *He made Him who knew no sin to be sin on our behalf, that we might become the righteousness of God in Him (II Corinthians 5:21).*

Consequently, God's wrath over sin does not have to be poured out upon us. The blood of Jesus enables us to have a totally new relationship with Him.

We are reconciled to God. His attitude toward us is one of amazing, unconditional love. Our attitude toward Him ought to be the same. When we accept His love—by acknowledging that Jesus paid the penalty for our sin with His blood, repenting of our sins, and seeking His forgiveness—we can be free from sin's deadly domination of our lives. Paul said:

. . . having now been justified by His blood, we shall be saved from the wrath of God through Him (Romans 5:9).

The great hymn writer Charles Wesley put it this way in his classic, "And Can It Be":

And can it be that I should gain
An int'rest in the Savior's blood?
Died He for me, who caused His pain?
For me, who Him to death pursued?
Amazing love! how can it be
That thou, my God, shouldst die for me?

ZOOM IN

1. Read Romans 5:1-11 in several different translations of the Bible. How does the blood of Jesus make your salvation possible?
2. Next time you get a paper cut on your finger, or some other minor injury, remind yourself of the horrible pain Jesus must have experienced as He paid the price for your sins by dying on the cross. Thank Him for His incredible, marvelous love. Of course, you don't have to wait until you cut yourself to thank Him!

in PROCESS

Pure as the Driven Slush

dr. Helen Roseveare, a medical missionary to Africa, related in her book, *Living Holiness,* a poignant story of Jaki, one of more than one hundred orphan children for whom she and other missionaries were caring at a mission compound in Kenya. It was lunchtime and the children were happily splashing their hands in the cool water pool, washing off the dirt and grime, excitedly anticipating the delicious meal God had provided and the mission workers had prepared. They paused to thank the Lord for the lunch, then the children began pressing forward toward the food line, but not before they passed inspection. Each child had to show that his or her hands were clean before being permitted to go through the line.

On this day, Jaki had not paid close enough attention to the cleansing process that was supposed to have taken place at the pool. As he hurriedly attempted to sneak through inspection, the voice of authority was heard to say, "Jaki, go and wash your hands!"

"But, Miss, I have washed them!"

"Jaki, look at them. They're filthy!"

"Please, Miss, I did wash them! I did; I truly did."

"Miss, he did," shouted a friend. "I saw him, down at the pool."

Authority was unimpressed.

"Jaki, just look at your hands. Are they clean?"

"But I washed. I washed. I really washed!" wailed Jaki.

"I merely asked you to look at your hands, and tell me if you think they are clean," was the patient reply of authority.

As Jaki turned to leave the line and make his way back to the water hole, he could be heard muttering, "But how clean do my hands have to be to be clean?"

<small>Adapted from *Living Holiness*, by Helen Roseveare, (Minneapolis: Bethany House Publishers, 1986), p. 43.</small>

Jaki's question hits the nail right on the head for most of us. How clean is clean? Better yet, how pure is pure?

The question is especially relevant because the Scriptures clearly state that if we are to know intimate communion with God, we must be clean, not just on the outside, but on the inside, as well. Perhaps that's why the psalmist pondered:

> *Who may ascend into the hill of the Lord?*
> *And who may stand in His holy place?*
> *He who has clean hands and a pure heart,*
> *Who has not lifted up his soul to falsehood,*
> *And has not sworn deceitfully (Psalm 24:3, 4).*

Who is going to see God? In the Beatitudes, Jesus said:

> *Blessed are the pure in heart, for they shall see God (Matthew 5:8).*

Pure in heart? Jesus, are You kidding? Who talks about purity these days? Who even thinks about purity in the kind of world in which we live? In a world where smut and perversion scream at us from our televisions and radios; where billboards belch antibiblical messages; where our moral values are repeatedly mauled and maligned in the magazines, movies, and music of our culture; in a world filled with moral filth and ethical degradation, who talks about purity? In a public school system where one out of two teenagers has already squandered away his or her virginity; where more than 50 percent of the students have experimented with drugs or alcohol and an overwhelming 75 percent cheat regularly on their tests; in such a world, who talks about purity?

And why shouldn't the kids cheat? They've been trained well by their parents. For years, the children have watched Mom and Dad cheat the salesclerks, cheat in business, cheat the Internal Revenue Service, and often cheat on each other. In a world where cheaters usually win, who talks about purity?

In a world where might makes right; where nice guys finish last, according to Leo Durocher; and where *Nice Guys Sleep Alone* according to Bruce Feirstein; in such a world as ours, who talks about purity anymore?

Who talks about purity?

God does.

His standards do not change with every wind and whim of our society. His commands remain solidly the same. He requires that I be morally blameless, that I be clean, pure, and spotless.

Now, that creates a serious problem for me. I mean, I know me! I am painfully aware of my failures and my sins, and I know that if forced to stand alone on my own goodness before God, I wouldn't stand a chance of entering heaven. Because, basically, apart from Jesus Christ, I am a sinful person.

You probably have the same problem. God says you are to be pure and you aren't. Your dilemma is further complicated because you know that it is absolutely impossible for you ever to become pure through your own efforts. Perhaps you have already tried that route—and failed. You know how it goes: Just when you think your hands are clean and your heart is pure, God shines His searchlight upon you, and the brilliance of His holiness discloses the dirt that you allowed to remain hidden in the shadows.

Disgusting, isn't it?

The apostle Paul must have experienced something similar. See if you can identify with his sentiments in Romans 7:15-25.

> *For that which I am doing, I do not understand; for I am not practicing what I would like to do, but I am doing the very thing I hate. . . . for the wishing is present in me, but the doing of the good is not. For the good that I wish, I do not do; but I practice the very evil that I do not wish. But if I am doing the very thing I do not wish, I am no longer the one doing it, but sin which dwells in me (Romans 7:15, 18-20).*

Paul saw the issues clearly. He was saying, "I'm supposed to be good, and yet I keep being bad. God knows I want to be pure, yet for all of my efforts, I remain impure, and there seems to be nothing I can do about it." I can identify with that; how about you?

There once was a little boy who constantly got into trouble. Everywhere he went, trouble seemed to follow him—at home, at school, even at church. His Sunday school teacher, however, was a paragon of virtue and the boy admired her immensely. One day as he was comparing his conduct to hers, he lamented with despair evident in his voice, "Teacher you're so good and I'm so bad. I just wish you could crawl down inside of me; then, I'd be good like you are!"

Though the youngster's theology leaves much to be desired, he unwittingly struck upon the secret to the Christian life. The key to positive, victorious, Christlike conduct is "Christ in you, the hope of glory" (Colossians 1:27b). Nowhere does the Word of God imply that successful Christian living depends upon your abilities, spiritual or otherwise. It is not you at your best attempting to live up to God's holiness. It all depends upon Him. Face it: You can't measure up to His standards. By rights, you deserve to die for what you have said, thought, and done. Furthermore, you cannot take away a single sin that you have ever committed.

But, thank God, Jesus can! Do you remember Paul's pointed question that came after his despondent description of his defeat in the face of sin? Paul cried out, ". . . Who will set me free from the body of this death?" Then, as though somebody had switched on a light bulb in his heart and mind, he suddenly perceived the answer to his own question: "Thanks be to God through Jesus Christ our Lord! . . ." (Romans 7:24, 25).

Paul saw that Jesus was his only hope of ever being acceptable to God. Christ in us is our only hope of glory.

ZOOM IN

1. Why do you think most of us have such a hard time being good?
2. If one of your best friends said, "Hey, I don't need Jesus to be good. I just need more willpower," how would you respond?
3. Today, acknowledge Jesus Christ as Lord of your life. Say the words aloud, "Jesus, I give my life totally into Your hands. Please cleanse me of sin, and give me the power of Your Holy Spirit to overcome sin's power in my life."

in PROCESS

So You Want to Be a Disciple

have you ever wondered why Jesus doesn't just go on national TV and say, "All right, you guys, listen up! I am the Messiah and you better believe in Me, or else"? Then He could do a world tour, or something. Well, maybe He wouldn't do it quite that way. . . .

But seriously, haven't you ever wondered about Jesus' approach to saving the world? Think about it. His goal was to get the Gospel to every person on the planet, and His primary method of spreading the Word was not to go on radio or TV, cut an album, or have a tape ministry. He recruited a few disciples, twelve to be exact, and one of them turned out to be a lemon.

Actually, the brilliance of Jesus' plan was to enlist men (and women later on) who would bear witness to His life and carry on His word long after He had returned to be with the Father in heaven.

The first guys Jesus chose (before He even preached a public sermon or performed a miracle) were called disciples. The word means "learners" or "pupils." They were to be students in Jesus' school of eternal life. The guys Jesus picked didn't have to be smart; they weren't required to be strong or good-looking. They didn't have to know how to sing or play an instrument, nor were they required to have a degree before they could follow the Master. But Jesus did expect the men who were part of His team to obey Him. They had to be willing to trust Him. Oh, yes; they had to be loyal, too. And they were—except for Judas. Until you get to the crucifixion accounts, nowhere in the Gospels do you read of any one of the disciples being disloyal to Jesus. That's one of the reasons no one suspected Judas of betraying Jesus.

Apparently, the disciples' reputation for commitment to their Lord was so strong, not even Caiaphas, the crafty high priest, could imagine one of them being corrupted. The Gospel writers specifically point out that Judas went to Jesus' enemies and offered to cut a deal; the chief priests, scribes, and Pharisees did not initially approach Judas (Matthew 26:14, 15; Mark 14:10; Luke 22:3-6). They would not have dreamed of doing so; the disciples' loyalty to Christ was unquestioned.

But even considering the total commitment of Jesus' disciples, why did He concentrate so much of His time on so few people? Especially after John the Baptist, the most radical (if not the most popular) preacher of the day had proclaimed Him as the Lamb of God, the One about whom he had been preaching and for whom he had been looking. Jesus could have capitalized on John's endorsement, mounted a Ross Perot-type, grass-roots campaign and swept into power before Herod, the reigning king, could have known what had hit him! But He didn't.

Why? Because Jesus was not trying to win a popularity contest. At times, it actually seemed as though Jesus purposely made it more difficult for people to follow Him. For example, the day after the feeding of the five thousand (John 6:1-15), Jesus began to spell out how a person could only come to know God through Him, and other difficult-to-accept truths (John 6:22-66). The crowd evaporated! The apostle John poignantly comments:

> *As a result of this many of His disciples withdrew, and were not walking with Him anymore (John 6:66).*

Jesus didn't mind. He was looking for men and women who would lead the multitude, not fickle followers who would fold at the first sign of pressure. He expected His followers to believe in Him (John 14:12, 13), and then He expected them to pass the word on to others, who in turn would spread the message to others, until the whole world might know who He was and what He came to do (Matthew 28:19, 20; John 15:13-27).

Jesus never promised that His disciples would be popular. Actually, He said just the opposite. On several occasions, Jesus told His disciples they should expect persecution. As "learners" of Him, He predicted people would oppose them at every turn. He said:

> *If the world hates you, you know that it has hated Me before it hated you. If you were of the world, the world would love its own; but because you are not of the world, but I chose you out of the world, therefore the world hates you. Remember the word that I said to you, "A slave is not greater than his master." If they persecuted Me, they will also persecute you; if they kept My word, they will keep yours also (John 15:18-20).*

True to Jesus' words, all of the disciples experienced persecution—real physical pain as well as verbal abuse—in their lives. All but John died violent deaths as martyrs, rather than be disloyal to Jesus. Furthermore, that has been the case down through history. Christians have had to pass through unspeakable tortures and trials for their faith. Yet no matter how much pressure was applied, they refused to renounce their commitment to Christ. (If you ever want to rid yourself of any ideas that Christianity is for sissies, pick up the book *Foxes' Book of Martyrs*. Just don't eat lunch before you begin reading.)

Today, Jesus' plan remains intact. He has no "plan B" to fall back upon. To His disciples, it was a definite command: "Go ye into all the world . . ." No one who followed Jesus for any length of time could escape that commission, nor did they try to do so. His command is just as binding upon His disciples today. He has called us to take the Gospel to the world, inch by inch, school by school, town by town, nation by nation. And He has promised to go with us, every step of the way.

ZOOM IN

1. Look again at what we call the Great Commission in Matthew 28:18-20 and Mark 16:14-18. Then flip back to Mark 8:34-38 to see what Jesus means when He talks about us being disciples.
2. Why do you think Jesus did not use His power to enlist a mighty army and take the world by storm? In a spiritual sense, how do you think He has done just that?
3. Today, why not begin to apply Jesus' strategies of personal evangelism and start working with a small group? Maybe you could form a Bible study with some of your friends.
4. Jesus expected His disciples to pick up His ways and teachings simply by being with Him. Is there anyone who can mentor you in your spiritual life, someone you can learn from just by being with him or her? Maybe your pastor or youth leader would allow you to follow him around for a day or two, to learn informally how he walks with God. Of course, the best way to learn about Jesus is to read your Bible and talk to Him in prayer, to spend time with Him.

in PROCESS
Signs of a Christian

A lot of people call themselves Christians nowadays. Unfortunately, the term "born again" has been so prostituted, it has lost most of its original meaning. How can you tell the difference between a real Christian and a fake? More importantly, how can you tell if you are the real thing?

The apostle Paul lists at least three marks of a true Christian in I Thessalonians 1:1-10. Take a minute to see if you can find them. (Hint: check out verses 9 and 10.)

Paul was writing to a group of new believers in Thessalonica, a town famous for its pagan idol worship. Paul had been able to personally instruct these new believers for only three weeks before he was forced to flee for his life. You can imagine how elated the apostle was when word came to him that the Thessalonians' conversions had been genuine, and despite persecutions, they were hanging in there with the Lord.

Three evidences convinced Paul that the Thessalonians were for real:

1. They had turned to God and away from their idols (vs. 9).
2. They were now serving the living and true God (vs. 9).
3. They were waiting for the return of Jesus Christ (vs. 10).

These new Christians realized they couldn't have Jesus and their idols, too. To wholeheartedly serve God, they had to do some housecleaning, which included getting rid of their idols.

Today when we think of idols, we tend to conjure up images of half-naked heathen poking pins in voodoo dolls in darkened jungles. But a lot of idol worshipers wear designer clothes and can be found in brightly lit classrooms, offices, and churches.

What is an idol? Anything that stands between you and God and takes the place that rightfully belongs to Jesus Christ in your life becomes an idol for you. It could be a good gift from God that you have allowed to take precedence over Him. It may be your girlfriend or boyfriend, your car, your academic or athletic ability, your job, your physical appearance, your family, or even your refrigerator (think about that one!). On the other hand, you may have allowed something destructive to become an idol. You could be worshiping an idol of drugs, alcohol, or cigarettes. Maybe you are bowing to an idol created by an inner attitude of lust, greed, or pride.

Whether your idol is a "good" thing or a "bad" thing is really irrelevant. If you are worshiping an idol, you are not worshiping Jesus. The first of the Ten Commandments is:

> *You shall have no other gods before Me. You shall not make for yourself an idol, or any likeness of what is in heaven above or on the earth beneath or in the water under the earth. You shall not worship them or serve them; for I, the Lord your God, am a jealous God (Exodus 20:3-5a).*

A second sign of a true Christian is a desire to serve the Lord. Notice, for example, not only did the Thessalonians turn from their lifeless, wooden, and stone idols, but they also began to serve the living and true God.

Sometimes you may wonder why God would want somebody like you to serve Him. Certainly, with a snap of His supernatural fingers, He could have 10,000 angels ready to do His will. And they wouldn't give Him any back talk about it either! Why would God want you to serve Him?

It's not that complicated, really. Are you ready for this? *God wants you to serve Him as an expression of your love for Him.* That's it. That sums it up. Jesus said:

> *You are My friends, if you do what I command you (John 15:14).*

He doesn't want you to serve Him out of fear that He is going to zap you with lightning if you don't. He knows love is something you do. You don't show your love for Christ with words alone; you show love by how you live for Him.

An amazing by-product of this type of service is joy. Jesus spelled it out this way:

> *If you keep My commandments, you will abide in My love; just as I have kept My Father's commandments, and abide in His love. These things I have spoken to you, that My joy may be in you, and that your joy may be made full (John 15:10, 11).*

If your main goal in life is not to love and serve God, you will experience constant tension and turmoil. You were made to love and serve the living and true God. When you do, you will find joy, happiness, peace, and a sense of meaning that comes from knowing you are doing what you were created to do.

When you live that way, waiting for the return of Jesus is not a dull, boring, treading-water type of life-style. Each day is an exciting adventure, filled with new opportunities to serve Him until He comes! Do something today that you know will make Jesus happy. You'll be happy you did.

ZOOM IN

1. Ask God to help you recognize and remove any idols that are taking His place in your heart.
2. What are some signs of true Christianity that you can see developing in your life?

in PROCESS

Where Is God in the Dark?

have you ever been in a brightly lit room when suddenly the electrical power has gone off? For a moment you stand there paralyzed, wondering, *What in the world is happening?* Then once you realize (or, at least you think you understand what has happened), you stretch your hands out in front of you and begin plodding slowly, ever so slowly, to where Mom keeps the candles and matches. Maybe, if you're lucky, you can find a flashlight.

It's a lonely, eerie feeling when the lights go out. It is even more disconcerting when the lights go out on your spiritual life. Do you know how it feels, like God has gone away somewhere and left you all alone in the dark? You sense a strange emptiness in your life. You read the Bible, but it seems as dry as dust. You pray, but it feels as though your prayers are getting stuck on the ceiling. *What's going on?* you wonder.

Where is God in the dark?

If you are "semi-spiritual," you begin examining your life. "Did I mess up somehow? Have I sinned? Have I not been praying or reading my Bible enough? Have I been hanging out with the wrong crowd?" A host of other questions cross your mind.

If you are really spiritual, you blame the darkness on the devil or his demons. But if you rebuke every demon you can think of and the darkness remains, then what?

The truth is that every godly person in the Bible, and every saint we know anything about down through church history, has experienced something similar. No true Christian lives a life of constant sunshine. We all have times of cold, hard, winter darkness. The saints of old called it "the dark night of the soul."

Believe it or not, sometimes God purposely allows those dark times in the lives of His people. For instance, we remember Moses as the man God used to deliver Israel from Egyptian bondage. But we tend to forget that Moses became so frustrated with the job God had called him to do, and the people with whom he had to live and work, that he asked God to kill him!

> *So Moses said to the Lord, "Why hast Thou been so hard on Thy servant? And why have I not found favor in Thy sight, that Thou hast laid the burden of all this people on me? . . . So if Thou art going to deal thus with me, please kill me at once, if I have found favor in Thy sight, and do not let me see my wretchedness" (Numbers 11:11, 15).*

Whew! Talk about depression and discouragement! Moses was really down in the dumps. Yet he sounds like a positive-thinking, motivational speaker compared to the Old Testament character, Job. When his world was crumbling and his body was being smitten by Satanic attack, Job cursed the day he was born (Job 3:1-3). That's what I call darkness of the soul!

Knowing that you are not the first person to ever go through spiritual darkness is comforting, but what should you do when those dark times come?

In his wonderfully warm, witty, and wisdom-filled book, *The Thomas Factor,* Winkie Pratney, a popular Bible teacher at many Christian festivals, offers some practical advice. Assuming you have already checked your life for willful disobedience and taken authority over any demonic attack, Winkie suggests:

1. **Do your duty nevertheless.** The main thing to do when the darkness comes, once you have gotten your bearings, is to maintain your direction. In other words, don't allow the darkness to ruin your day (or week, or month, or year!).

    What was God doing in your life before you went into the darkness? What was your call when you could clearly hear the voice of God? Whatever it was, keep doing it! You may have to proceed a bit more slowly and pick your way more carefully, but stay on the path and keep moving forward.

2. **Keep trusting.** In our church, we often sing a praise chorus based on Proverbs 18:10, "The name of the Lord is a strong tower; the righteous runs into it and is safe." When the lights go out, it is important to keep trusting and singing His name. Remember, the Lord's name is "I AM." He is, whether you can feel His presence or not. The darkness doesn't change Him. But when you don't feel Him near you, that is an excellent time to declare, "Lord, I believe in You. Whether I feel Your presence or not, I believe You are here with me in the darkness."

3. **Recall what God has done.** Think about how God has blessed your life in the past and thank Him for those blessings. Remind yourself of those things He has done for others, too—your friends, family members, other Christians you've heard about or read about.

    Look up passages in the Bible that have been especially meaningful to you in your walk with God.

    Acknowledge who He is and your commitment to Him. Sometimes, real spiritual power is released merely by verbalizing what you believe: "I know who You are, Lord, and I believe in You. I have seen You move in the past, and I commit myself to trusting You now and in the future."

    Adapted from Winkie Pratney, *The Thomas Factor* (Old Tappan, N.J.: Chosen Books, Fleming H. Revell Co., 1989), pp. 165-168.

The best part about struggling though the darkness is what happens when the power lines are repaired. Suddenly, the room bursts with light, and the brightness is nearly blinding. So it is in your walk with God. When you've been in the darkness for a while, you learn to appreciate the light in a new way.

Not only that, you realize, "Hey, God really has blessed me with a bunch of light already!" When you come out of the darkness, you'll have a greater sense of God's light than when you went in—and that alone is worth it.

ZOOM IN

1. Today, turn to Isaiah 50:10, 11. Notice that even those who fear the Lord sometimes must walk in a God-imposed darkness. Also, don't miss the Lord's emphasis on the fact that He is the only One who can bring us out of the darkness into the light.
2. The pupils of our "spiritual eyes" often grow so accustomed to the light, our perception of the world shrinks to the size of a dot. It is only when we step out of the darkness into the light that we can appreciate the light the Lord has already revealed to us. Today, be sure to thank the Lord for teaching you how to walk in His light (I John 1:7).
3. Jesus had His "dark night of the soul" in the Garden of Gethsemane, the night before He went to the cross (Luke 22:39-44). His prayer was:

   Father, if Thou art willing, remove this cup from Me; yet not My will, but Thine be done (vs. 42).

   When you are going through dark times, make Jesus' prayer your own.
4. No matter what you go through, God has promised that He will be there with you. Check out a few of these Scripture promises and let your heart well up with hope! Joshua 1:9; Psalm 42:11; Psalm 138:7, 8; Isaiah 40:31; John 14:27; II Corinthians 4:8,14; Philippians 4:6, 7.

in PROCESS

Jesus Is Everything to Me

people often ask me how I write a song. That's a tough question to answer, because there are no pat formulas; our creative God inspires creativity in various ways. I've found that my main role in songwriting is to stay open to whatever fresh and exciting ways He may inspire me.

Sometimes He gives me ideas for songs in the middle of the night. At other times, the Lord will bring an idea to mind as Gary and I are riding down the highway. And some days I wake up and think, "Today, my job is to write a song."

All of these songwriting methods are equally inspired of God. When I first began writing songs, I believed the only songs that were truly blessed by God were the ones that came through some dramatic "revelation." I have since discovered that God honors discipline and hard work, too.

Sometimes songs just seem to come to life by themselves, but at other times I have to labor and pray over every syllable. Some songs take a few minutes to write; others take hours, days, weeks, and sometimes even months. In one sense, every song takes years to write because each, in some way, is an expression of my spiritual experience to date. The longer I journey with Jesus, the more I want to sing about what He is teaching me. A song from my "Facts of Love" album is a great example of how the Lord brings the process together.

Gary and I had gone to visit some friends of ours, Trace Scarborough and Scott MacLeod. The guys let us listen to a

Jesus is everything to me

rough mix of some demo tracks they had cut but hadn't written any words to yet. They played five or six tracks for us, and the moment I heard the last one, I shouted, "That's it! That's exactly what I've been looking for!"

Trace and Scott gave me a cassette copy to take with me. As Gary and I were driving home, I knew I wanted to call the song, "Everything." By the time we pulled into our driveway, the Lord was pouring ideas into my heart and mind.

I went into our home office and shut the door. I sat down on the floor and started writing some of the many things the Lord has done for me and how He has been everything to me. Before long, tears began trickling down my cheeks. The Lord's presence was so real in that room! When I saw on paper, in my own handwriting, the many things the Lord has done in, through, and for me, it became almost overwhelming. I continued to sense His anointing and scribbled lyrics on tear-stained paper.

I wrote many more things than I could possibly squeeze into one song, things such as:

When I needed a friend, He was a friend who stuck closer than a brother.
When I needed a companion, He was there.
He's never left me or forsaken me.
When I needed power, He supplied it.
Greater is He who is in me than He who is in the world!
When I needed love, He gave it to me. Greater love hath no man than he lay down his life for a friend.

About thirty minutes later, the song had practically written itself. Here are some of the lyrics that mean so much to me:

Here's a little story / About a lonely girl
Nobody to talk to / Alone in this old world.
Out of desperation / Fell down on her knees
In case you haven't noticed / The lonely girl was me.
Don't know how I lived without Him for so long.

55

All I had to do was open up my heart.

Ain't no doubt about it / I can't live without Him.
He's everything, everything
I might have to shout it / Tell the world about Him
He's everything everything.

Lily of the valley / Bright and shining star
Baby in a manger / Lover of my heart
King of all creation / Knew my deepest need
In my darkest hour / He reached out to me.

Jesus is everything . . .
Jesus is all that I need.

> (By Kim Boyce / Scott MacLeod / Trace Scarborough; © 1992 Howlin' Hits Music, Inc./ Koreiba Music / Ocean Music; Used by permission. All rights reserved.)

Shortly after the song came out on the radio, it zoomed to the number one spot on the charts. That's a neat feeling, but even more gratifying were the comments I received from people in our own church who said, "Hey, Kim. I heard 'Everything' on the radio and it really ministered to me."

To me, that's what writing songs is all about!

ZOOM IN

1. Whatever you are going through right now, some aspect of Jesus' personality is exactly what you need. Whether you are going through trials and tribulations or celebrating a triumph, He will be there with you. Write down some of the things Jesus has done for you. Be sure to thank Him!
2. To get a better idea of who Jesus wants to be in your life, read Isaiah 9:6, 7; Matthew 1:21-23, and John 1:29-34. Notice the various descriptions of Jesus. List the things He impresses upon your heart that He has promised to be to you.

in PROCESS | *Self-Portrait*

in PROCESS
Unique or You're Not

Sometimes fitting in gets to be a bit bewildering. You have to really know what's in and what's out, what's hot and what's not. Steve, a high school senior, summed up the spirit of the times: "No matter what, you've got to look like you belong, like you know what's happenin'. To be avoided at all costs is looking, acting, or talking like someone who just came in from out of town."

Amazing, isn't it? In an age when we are crying out against conformity and sameness, idolizing our individuality, those of the so-called "in crowd" are still trying to establish their identity by fitting into somebody else's ideas of how they should look, act, or talk. Maybe the strangest thing is that since political correctness and the androgynous look came along, we are all starting to sound and look somewhat the same, more or less a monotonous community of clones. For all our talk about self-expression and personal freedom, we have become boringly banal.

Most of us are more comfortable and secure when we fit into the crowd. "If my buddy does it, I'll do it too. But if he (or she) won't, I'm out of here."

Many modern-day youth won't even raise their hands in class to answer a question—not because they don't know the answer, but because their self-images have been so battered, they are reluctant to venture even that far out on their own. In most classrooms, the students sit in their cliques, looking like plaster of Paris statues that have been propped up in the chairs. The teacher can be good or bad; it hardly matters. The class won't even blink.

They're laid-back, uncommitted, bland and blasé, obligated by peer pressure to look bored, even if they are not. If Jeff the Jock, sitting in the corner with his feet propped up on the chair in front of him, finds something funny and lets out a laugh, the other kids might laugh too—but not until. Or, if Glamorous Geena groans, several other students will groan with her—but not until.

Sound familiar? What's really sad is that most of these young men and women are not ignorant or disinterested. On the contrary, kids nowadays are some of the brightest, sharpest young people ever! It's just that many of them have had their self-esteem so beaten into the ground, they won't even attempt to express themselves in a group of more than two or three friends.

Their credo is, "Let somebody else stick out his (or her) neck—not me!" Their philosophy is sort of like the old cowboys-and-Indians method of research: If you send out a scout and he comes back shot full of arrows, you say, "Well, I guess that's not a good place to be!"

Nobody wants to take responsibility if things don't pan out just right. People would rather sit back and wait for someone else to tell them what to do. "Follow the leader" is no longer merely a childhood game. For many young men and women, it has become a way of life. The leader may be the local sports hero, the local pothead, or the latest pop-music flame. It is to such demagogues that some of your friends and mine are willing to abdicate their decision making, thrusting it into the oftentimes incompetent hands of the personality with the highest profile, or the person whose promises sound the most like what they want to hear.

Some individualism, huh? That's not being unique or different; that's conformity. And it is conformity of the most demeaning sort—simply acquiescing to the clamor of the crowd. Keep your mouth shut, go with the flow . . . and become a nonperson.

That's one of the reasons I am a Christian. Christians are different. Not weird—different. Perhaps the most liberating part of the Good News is that you don't have to be just like everyone else in order to "fit in." As a Christian, you can be free from all that! You are set apart from the maddening masses and can go against the flow when necessary.

You don't have to derive your sense of self-worth from society's status symbols or from what anyone else says you should be or do in order to have value. God thought you were important enough and of such immense value, that He gave His only Son, Jesus, to die on Calvary's cross, so you might be free—really free!

Furthermore, He will give you the courage and strength to fight against the tide of conformity. Believe it or not, the Holy Spirit will even help you to buck the system when it tempts you to live contrary to God's Word.

Many Christians are "blown away" when they discover that God never intended for them to be like everybody else. In fact, the omnipotent Creator, the ultimate source of creativity, despises our attempts to attach tags and labels to people and our efforts to squeeze His diverse, original creations into the same container. It just won't work.

Maybe that's one reason the apostle Paul wrote:

> *Do not be conformed to this world, but be transformed by the renewing of your mind, that you may prove what the will of God is, that which is good and acceptable and perfect (Romans 12:2).*

This passage is one of my favorites in the entire Bible. It helps me to be me, not some image that others think I ought to be. At least two obvious principles spring from Paul's instructions:

In process

1. Don't be conformed to this world! You are unique, so you can dare to be different; dare to be yourself!
2. Be transformed by the renewing of your mind. Allow God to renew your mental attitude and self-image according to His Word. And dare to live your life according to the picture He has given you, not by what anyone else says.

ZOOM IN

1. Has there ever been a time when you felt inferior because you felt you didn't fit in? Maybe you weren't dressed "right" or weren't able to buy your clothes at the "right" store. Flip open your Bible to Matthew 6:25-33 and consider how your experience relates to this passage.
2. What are some qualities about you that make you distinctly different from anyone else? Write at least three of those characteristics on a small piece of paper and carry it with you today. As you get a chance, pull out your list, and say something like, "Thanks, Lord, for making me who I am, the way I am."

in PROCESS
Shirley's Secret

Everyone who knew her thought Shirley had her life all together. Nobody could have imagined that she was walking around with a severely wounded self-image—the result of her childhood memories.

Shirley grew up in a run-down house with no yard in which to play. Several of the walls in her family's house had gaping holes where her drunken father had hammered his fists in fits of anger. Shirley was so embarrassed by the condition of her home that she refused to invite her friends to visit. She knew their houses didn't have holes in the walls. Her self-esteem plummeted through the floor.

Her dad's drinking problem exacerbated the already existing tension between Shirley's parents. Maybe that's why her mom decided to send little Shirley and her brother to Sunday school. Shirley's mom knew she needed all the help she could get in raising the children.

At Sunday school, Shirley's young, impressionable mind began to grasp the truth about Jesus Christ. Her Sunday school teacher told the class, "God loves all of you, and He knows each of your names." For a little girl who felt like a nobody, that was incredibly good news!

Shirley began memorizing Scripture. She wanted to learn more about this God who loved her. The first verse her Sunday school teacher taught her was:

> *In my Father's house are many mansions: if it were not so, I would have told you. I go to prepare a place for you (John 14:2, KJV).*

Shirley could hardly believe it! In her earthly father's house, all she had known was embarrassment, fighting, and alcohol-induced anger. But in her heavenly Father's house, Jesus was preparing a place especially for her, a place where she would never be embarrassed to invite her friends! Shirley committed her life to Jesus Christ, and asked Him to forgive her for all her sins. She vowed to live for Him the rest of her life.

Unfortunately, Shirley's parents continued to have troubles in their marriage. Her dad was unfaithful to her mom, and they ended up getting a divorce. Because of his problems with alcohol, Shirley's dad had never been able to do much to bolster his daughter's self-esteem. Now what little support he had given her was gone.

About that time, Shirley decided to ask God for a special favor. She got down on her knees and asked the Lord to send a Christian man for her mom to marry and to be a father to her and her brother. A year later, Shirley's mom met a wonderful Christian man who eventually became Shirley's stepdad. Shirley was ecstatic over her new father, not only because he loved her mom, but also because he was a physical confirmation of Shirley's faith in her heavenly Father!

Buoyed up by her answer to prayer, Shirley boldly began making another request of the Lord. She prayed that God would give her a Christian husband when the time came for her to get married. Eight years later, after Shirley had graduated from high school and was attending Pasadena College, God brought the answer to her childhood prayers. He was six foot two, blond-haired, captain of the tennis team, and he had plans to become a psychologist. Most important of all to Shirley, he was a dedicated Christian with an unshakable faith in Jesus. His name was Jim. Jim Dobson. As in Dr. James Dobson, now known around the world as the president of Focus on the Family, and host of the radio program of the same name.

Shirley and Jim dated for three years before they got married, which gave them plenty of time to get to know one another and build a firm spiritual foundation in their relationship before marriage. Undoubtedly, that is one of the reasons their marriage remains strong after more than twenty years.

As for Shirley Dobson's battle with her self-esteem, the Lord has brought healing there, as well. It started several years after they were married, when Dr. Dobson asked Shirley to share her testimony with a Sunday school class of young married couples he was teaching at their church. Shirley reluctantly agreed. It was one of the most difficult things she had ever done.

Nevertheless, Shirley opened up and began sharing from her heart some of the hurts from her childhood. As she did, the Lord began a marvelous work of inner healing in Shirley and in others in the class, many of whom had been holding onto resentments toward their parents. Not only did God set Shirley free from the past, but He used her experiences to help others find freedom as well.

Today, take a look at the whole passage of Scripture containing the verse that meant so much to Shirley Dobson—John 14:1-15. The Lord loves you, and He knows you by name; and yes, He is preparing a home for you in heaven that is going to be out of this world!

> Shirley's story is adapted from the book *Living Cameos*, by Helen Kooiman Hosier (Old Tappan, N.J.: Fleming H. Revell Co., 1984), pp. 31-33.

ZOOM IN

1. What qualities in your parents would you like to see reproduced in your children?
2. Perhaps your relationship with your earthly mother or father has had its shortcomings. It will do you no good to

harbor bitterness, resentment, or hatred. It's time to forgive any wrongs, repair any breaks in your relationship if possible, and then move on with your life. Don't allow your past experiences to keep you from loving and trusting your heavenly Father in the present. He will never run out on you, and He always has your best interests at heart.

3. Certainly, the Lord can heal instantaneously if He chooses to do so, but healing of emotional wounds suffered in childhood often takes some time. Frequently, the Lord uses other people, particularly pastors and professional Christian counselors, to help us take out the garbage from our pasts. Regardless of how He chooses to set you free, you have His Word that He will.

If therefore the Son shall make you free, you shall be free indeed (John 8:36).

4. God knows what is best for us, and He knows who is best for us too! If you are praying about your future mate, please, please be patient. I know it's not easy—I was in my late twenties when I met Gary—but I'm glad I waited for God's best in my life. You will be glad, too, when God gives His best to you!

in PROCESS

Where Did Daddy Go?

Ed Mortenson was born and raised in Norway, where he grew up to be a professional baker. He became successful enough to have his own bakery. Ed got married and had three children, but he refused to ever settle down and commit himself to his marriage or his children. After a few years, he walked out on his family, leaving them to fend for themselves in Norway. Eventually, Ed made his way to the United States.

Once in the U.S., Ed continued to earn his keep as a baker, but still he would not commit himself to any one woman. Then he met Gladys.

Gladys was a young woman whose husband had deserted her. Too bad she fell in love with Ed, a guy with a long history reflecting his lack of commitment. They didn't get married, but they began sleeping together, and before long the inevitable happened. Gladys got pregnant.

When Gladys told Ed that she was carrying their baby, the Norwegian baker simply stared at her and said nothing.

Gladys suggested that they go ahead and get married and give their child a decent home. After all, she and Ed were both working. Together, she just knew they could make it.

Ed continued to stare at her. He never answered a word. Finally, he turned around, walked out the door, got on his motorcycle, and rode away. He never came back and Gladys never saw his face again.

Ed traveled the country, moving from one town to the next, leaving a trail of broken hearts everywhere he went. He knew he had a child somewhere, although he wasn't certain of its sex, hair color, or anything else. In his more mellow moments, Ed sometimes thought it might be nice to meet his offspring someday. That day never came. On June 18, 1929, on a road near Youngstown, Ohio, Ed tried to pass a car with his motorcycle. An oncoming automobile hit him head-on. He died a few hours later at the hospital.

His child, carried by a mother whose husband had run out on her and whose "lover" had done the same, was a girl. She never knew the love of her daddy. Maybe that's why she engaged in numerous sexual affairs, posed nude in *Playboy* magazine, and would do almost anything to gain the love and affection of an admiring man. Her name was originally Norma Jean, but you probably know her best by the name she made famous . . . Marilyn. Marilyn Monroe.

Marilyn Monroe is certainly not the only person whose difficulties in life can be traced back to a missing father. Myriad men and women today feel worthless and unloved because they grew up without the guidance of a father. Worse yet, many have difficulty relating to God as their heavenly Father simply because they cannot imagine their own earthly father being there for them. Or they project onto God all the character flaws of their own earthly fathers. Maybe their dad criticized or punished them unjustly, unfairly, or too harshly. Consequently, they feel God the Father is an overbearing, judgmental bully of a God whom they can never satisfy. They feel that no matter what they do, it won't be good enough.

Others feel the pain of being abandoned or rejected by their earthly fathers. Some, of course, lost out on their relationships with their fathers because of death or divorce. Still others feel that Dad was always so busy with work, or so tired after work, there never seemed to be anything left for the kids. They were consistently disappointed by their dads throughout their growing-up years. As a result, many young men and women refuse to trust a Father-God; they won't even give Him a chance.

Yet one of the clearest revelations in the Bible is that God is our heavenly Father. He offers us protection, provision, warmth, tenderness, forgiveness, and yes, consistency. He is there for us.

If you have trouble relating to God because of the failure or absence of one or both of your parents during your childhood, please understand; the Lord loves you and He longs to spend time with you. He will never walk out on you, never desert you. He even put it in writing:

> *I will never desert you, nor will I ever forsake you. . . . I am with you always, even to the end of the age (Hebrews 13:5b; Matthew 28:20).*

Take a few moments to read the Lord's attitude toward you in the Old Testament passage, Hosea 11:3-9. The prophet's words are spoken on behalf of God the Father. Notice the unconditional love and affection He has for you, as well as His willingness to provide for you.

If your earthly father didn't provide for you or wasn't there for you, this may be hard to believe. Just remember though, your earthly father is human and very fallible; God, your heavenly father, is perfect. His love for you is perfect and never ending. You can bank your eternity on that!

ZOOM IN

1. Take a minute to read Psalm 68:5, 6. It says that God is a "father of the fatherless." What do you think that means?
2. If you have been hindered in your relationship with God by some failure of your parents, you must find forgiveness in your heart toward whoever hurt you. That's not easy, but if you ask the Lord to help you forgive those who hurt you, He will. Remember,

forgiveness is a choice, not a feeling.
3. God is the "Perfect Parent," but many of our images of God are caricatures or outlandish sketches, twisted and often terribly distorted representations. Get the real picture by seeing Him in His Word. Here are several references to help you get started: Psalm 103:13; Proverbs 3:11, 12; I Peter 5:7; I John 1:5.
4. Your heavenly Father loves you unconditionally. Nothing you have done—or ever will do—can cause Him not to love you. You are a priority on God's "daily planner." Think about that; let it just sink in.

in PROCESS
Just Be Yourself!

have you been to Wendy's lately? The next time you stop by for a burger or a Frosty at one of Wendy's nearly four thousand restaurants, thank God for the food . . . literally. Dave Thomas, founder of the chain named for his red-haired daughter, Wendy, claims that part of the reason he went into the restaurant business was he felt that "feeding folks" was the work God had called him to do. Apparently Dave made the right decision, because Wendy's now takes in over $3 billion a year from "feeding folks"!

What's his secret to success?

"Just be yourself," says Dave.

The chief executive officer and star of Wendy's television commercials obviously loves to eat, and his love for food is contagious. The commercials work. People believe him when they see him on their TV screens. But the commercials almost didn't happen.

The idea for Dave to appear in the commercials all started when the founder of Wendy's invited the company's advertising agency to visit him in his office so they could learn more about his values and how Wendy's operates. The company and the ad agency had a tough task ahead of them in their quest for a new advertising spokesperson. Clara Peller, the elderly woman who starred in the "Where's the beef?" commercials that captured the hearts of television audiences throughout the mid-1980s, had died. Two years

in process

later the company still hadn't found anyone able to fill Clara's tiny shoes.

As Dave Thomas explained his philosophy of fast food service to the ad executives, he was so enthusiastic that the agency representatives suggested he appear in the commercials himself! At first Dave thought they were kidding. He had never enjoyed the limelight; he was comfortable being a "behind the scenes" sort of guy. "After all," he jokes, "I'm a grill man who got a couple of breaks along the way and made the most of them. In fact, if some kind people hadn't adopted me as a baby, I don't know where I'd be today."

Dave grew up in Knoxville, Tennessee, and got his first job at the age of twelve, working (where else?) at the counter of a restaurant. He opened his first Wendy's in 1969. But in all of his life, he had never dreamed of going in front of a television camera to pitch burgers.

The ad agency execs, however, finally succeeded in convincing Dave to give it a try. "It will be easy," they said. "Dave, just be yourself."

Like most people who are unaccustomed to working on TV or doing videos, Dave Thomas quickly discovered that "being himself" wasn't as easy as he thought it would be. After ten attempts at the first commercial spot, the producers told him he needed "more energy . . . but just be yourself." Then they told him he needed to talk faster. "No, that doesn't work, talk slower. Look this way; no, look that way. Just be yourself, Dave."

Although Dave Thomas is an extremely confident person under normal circumstances, he soon became tongue-tied on the commercial set. In trying desperately to do a good job pitching Wendy's taco salad, an item Dave was genuinely enthusiastic about, he blurted, "Muchas gracy!" instead of, "Muchas gracias!" His next attempt was worse. After telling everyone how wonderful his new taco salad was, he declared, "Macho grassy!" The ad execs didn't think comparing the salad to strong grass would sell.

Just be yourself!

Four hours later, Dave still hadn't gotten the hang of "being himself" on camera. Finally, the director called for a break. Dave came off the set, sat down, and wiped the sweat off his forehead. "Being himself" was exhausting work! As he rested during the break, Dave began to think of Colonel Sanders, the Kentucky colonel of Kentucky Fried Chicken fame. He wasn't an actor; he was just a guy who believed that he had the greatest chicken going. He was a natural pitching his chicken, because he believed so much in the product.

As Dave mulled things over in his mind, he recalled a verse of Scripture, Isaiah 64:8:

> *But now, O Lord, Thou art our Father, we are the clay, and Thou our potter; and all of us are the work of Thy hand.*

"To me," Thomas said, "that means we have to accept ourselves as we are and be grateful for the way He made us."

Dave decided in doing the next commercial he was going to forget acting, and just be himself, no matter what. And he did! Dave Thomas began to relax, and as a result he became more natural; he became "himself." Ironically, when he started being himself he began focusing on "the other guy." He became less self-conscious and less tongue-tied. Instead of thinking about the cameras and the millions of dollars the company was spending on this commercial and the tens of millions of people who would see it, Dave began focusing on one man, the director. He talked directly to the director, making eye contact with him, trying to please only him. The end result was a convincing message to the world.

Have you ever tried to fit into somebody else's preconceived notions of how you should look, act, or talk? Pretty futile, isn't it? And frightening, too! In the Bible is an account of a young man who nearly lost his head because of trying to fit into somebody else's armor. His name was Dave too. You can find him "being himself," in I Samuel 17:20-51.

73

Saul probably meant well by offering David his armor. And it made a lot of sense to protect oneself as much as possible when going out to fight a giant. But it just wasn't right for David. His trust wasn't in armor or swords or even in stones. Notice his declaration to Goliath:

> *. . . You come to me with a sword, a spear, and a javelin, but I come to you in the name of the Lord of hosts. . . . This day the Lord will deliver you up into my hands . . . that all the earth may know that there is a God in Israel, and that all this assembly may know that the Lord does not deliver by sword or by spear; for the battle is the Lord's and He will give you into our hands (I Samuel 17:45-47).*

Today, in the face of whatever giants you are battling, just be yourself. Use whatever gifts and talents God has given you; use them in dependence upon Him—and for His great glory—and the giants will fall before you. Remember: The battle is the Lord's!

ZOOM IN

1. Dave Thomas was much more effective in getting his message across when he quit worrying about himself and focused on the director. How might remembering that help you be a better witness for Christ?
2. There's nothing wrong with using someone else's armor if it fits you. You can learn from others, use their plans, and incorporate their teachings in your life. But ultimately, you must find what God has for you to do in the way He wants you to do it.
   Today, pray something like this, "Lord, help me know Your will for my life. I believe You have given me certain gifts and abilities. I want to use those talents to glorify Your name. Show me the way, and I will walk in it."

in PROCESS
How to Be a Name-Dropper

a friend of Gary's and mine is a name-dropper. He is always talking about the latest star he has met in the music business, or how he was just talking to a certain person in Hollywood the other day, or that he knows this famous person or that famous person. He really does know some interesting, "big name" celebrities and other important people who have pull, power, prestige, or a lot of clout in the eyes of the world. But who cares?

Basically, our friend is an extremely insecure person, hoping to gain respect simply on the basis of his association with people more well-known than he is. Anyone who listens to his drivel usually does so only to hear some tidbit of information about somebody else. Few people seem to talk to our friend for the sake of learning more about him.

In most cases, name-dropping doesn't impress anyone. On the contrary, it is frequently offensive and is a fast way to become branded as a loser. However, there are two guys in the Bible who dropped a name and turned an entire city upside down. Check out their story in Acts 3:1-16.

Peter and John were going to the temple at about three o'clock in the afternoon. As they approached the temple gate known as "The Beautiful Gate," a crippled beggar began calling out to them, asking for money. The Beautiful Gate was one of the busiest entrances to the temple area; no doubt, the crippled man purposely positioned himself there every day so

75

he could be seen and heard by the most people, and hopefully, play on their sympathies as they approached the house of God. But he got more than he was begging for this day.

Peter looked him right in the eye and said, "Look at us!" The man gave Peter and John his undivided attention, assuming they were going to give him some money. But Peter surprised him when he said:

> *I do not possess silver and gold, but what I do have I give to you: In the name of Jesus Christ the Nazarene—walk! (Acts 3:6).*

Whew! Talk about name-dropping; Peter dropped an atomic bomb! Or at least it must have seemed like it to the poor crippled beggar, because suddenly he began to feel the strength coming back into his feet and his ankles. He literally jumped to his feet and began walking and leaping and praising God! When the people passing by saw the man and recognized him as the crippled beggar who usually sat outside the gate, they were amazed. Soon a crowd began to gather, so Peter, always the opportunist—his motto must have been "carpe diem," which means "seize the day"—started to preach. Shooting straight from the hip, he blasted his Jewish listeners.

He told them:

> *Men of Israel, why do you marvel at this, or why do you gaze at us, as if by our own power or piety we had made him walk? (Acts 3:12).*

Peter went on to tell them that it was the power of Jesus that had healed the man. He reminded them that this Jesus was the same person they had delivered up, disowned, and put to death.

Then Peter really surprised his audience by saying:

> *. . . the one whom God raised from the dead, a fact to which we are witnesses. And on the basis of faith in His name, it is the name of Jesus which has strengthened this man whom you see and know; and the faith which comes through Him has given him this perfect health in the presence of you all (Acts 3:15, 16).*

Did you notice the secret here? The supernatural power is in the name of Jesus, which represents the person of Jesus. A lot of people say the name of Jesus, but they don't have faith in the person of Christ. Consequently, nothing much happens (although that person may be guilty of using Christ's name in vain). Even repeating the phrase "in the name of Jesus" in your prayers will be fruitless if you don't believe Jesus can do what you are asking. But when you address any situation in the name of Jesus, which means "by the authority and power of Jesus Christ," a blast of His supernatural power is released into those circumstances, to destroy the works of the devil and to bring honor and glory to the name of Jesus Christ.

Now, that's what I call name-dropping!

ZOOM IN

1. Why do you think the name of Jesus carries so much power and authority?
2. Some people curse using the name of Jesus. Why do you think they do that? When they get angry and curse, why don't they say "Oh, Mohammed!" or "Oh, Buddha!" or "Oh, Hare Krishna?"
3. Why do you think some Christians use the name of Jesus and yet never seem to see any results?
4. The name of Jesus is the most powerful, authoritative name in heaven and on earth. To see why, read Philippians 2:9-11.

in PROCESS: *Wide-Angle Lens*

in PROCESS
God and Politics

Any good student of history can tell you that the driving force behind Great Britain's abolition of slavery in 1833 was William Wilberforce. But few secular historians will tell you what compelled Wilberforce to fight against overwhelming opposition for most of his adult life. The great political reformer was carrying out his commitment to Jesus Christ.

William Wilberforce had established himself as a powerful voice in British politics before he ever met Jesus Christ. Then, as a new Christian, Wilberforce sought counsel from a local pastor. The pastor had led a wild life himself and had worked aboard a slave ship prior to his conversion. At one point, he had even commanded his own slave ship. He knew firsthand the demeaning horrors of slavery. Then, during a storm-tossed trip to the West Indies, the slave trader had cried out for Jesus to save him, not just from the raging sea, but from the raging demons within himself. John Newton was converted to Christ and became a pastor. He is probably best known for the hymn he wrote expressing the joy and wonder of his salvation. You probably know at least part of the song by heart. It's called "Amazing Grace."

By the time William Wilberforce went to see Newton, the wily pastor had earned a reputation for speaking out against slavery and other injustices. He advised Wilberforce to follow Christ, not out of the political arena, but into it. Wilberforce heeded Newton's advice, and the world is a different place as a result.

But that was more than 160 years ago. Can a Christian still put his or her faith to work in politics and government within our pluralistic society? Why not?

Where did we ever get the idea that Christians should not run for political office or should not become involved in political campaigns? That idea certainly didn't come from God! Where does it say in your Bible that Christians should keep quiet in the face of abortion, euthanasia, racial prejudice, public immorality, and a host of other social issues that plague our society? Granted, we are to obey the law, but when man's laws violate God's laws, we have a responsibility to challenge them.

In his book *Kingdoms in Conflict,* Charles Colson provides an excellent assessment of the problems facing Christians in the political arena. Colson is well qualified to speak on the opportunities and pitfalls of politics. Prior to his conversion to Christ, Colson served as presidential counsel to Richard M. Nixon. Colson spent seven months in federal prison for his involvement in the Watergate scandal that brought the Nixon presidency to an end. Out of that, however, Colson and his wife found Jesus Christ. Since then, Colson has founded Prison Fellowship, a ministry that shares the love of Jesus with those behind bars and shows them how to be truly rehabilitated—from the inside out.

Because of his past experiences with political power and his current commitment to Jesus Christ, Chuck Colson possesses some keen insights concerning Christians in politics. Colson believes there are at least three compelling reasons Christians absolutely must be involved in politics and government. First, as citizens of this country, Christians have a duty to serve on juries, pay taxes, vote, and support candidates they think are best qualified. Second, as citizens of the kingdom of God, Christians are to bring God's standards of righteousness and justice to bear on the kingdoms of this world. Third, Christians have an obligation to bring moral values to the public's attention. Colson says, "All law involves morality; the popular idea that 'you can't legislate morality' is a myth. Morality is legislated every day from the vantage point of one value system or another. The question is not whether we will legislate morality, but whose morality we will legislate" (Charles Colson, *Kingdoms in Conflict,* Grand Rapids, Mich., Zondervan Publishing House, 1987, pp. 278-279).

For an example of how a believer can exercise godly principles in a heathen government, loaded with political intrigue, read Daniel 6:1-28. You will recognize this as the account of when Daniel joined "The Lions' Club," but it is worth reading again.

Daniel was about thirteen years of age when he was taken captive and exiled as a slave to King Nebuchadnezzar's Babylon. Soon, Daniel's captors recognized his God-given abilities and placed him in training to become—of all things—an administrator in Nebuchadnezzar's pagan empire! For the next seventy-some years (many Bible scholars believe Daniel was in his mid-eighties when he was cast into the lions' den), Daniel worked within an ungodly governmental system, yet did not compromise his faith in God or his moral and ethical integrity.

If that was possible in ancient Babylon, the land known today as Iraq, it is certainly possible within our governmental systems. But let's not be naïve. If you as a Christian hope to serve the Lord in government or in politics, you can expect to spend some time in a modern-day den of lions. No doubt there will be many vicious, sharp-toothed (and sharp-tongued) lions lying in wait for you. Does that mean you should avoid getting involved? On the contrary; you must take a stand for what is right according to God's standards.

Just as God raised Daniel to a position of prominence within the government, I believe He is searching for young men and women today who will serve Him at all levels of local, state, and national government. But remember, God is searching for servants, not professional politicians. He is calling His people to take His values not just into the church, but into the world.

ZOOM IN

1. What is an area of influence in which you feel strongly about becoming involved? No fair saying "I don't want to get involved." As Christians, we are called to obey God, and that involves representing Him to the world around us. The only questions are where, when, and how?
2. Keep in mind that not every Christian can be involved in every issue. Do what the Lord lays upon your heart to do, but please don't "look down your nose" self-righteously at those whose passion is not the same as yours or is expressed in different ways.
3. Social activism must never be viewed as an alternative to prayer, worship, evangelism, and other Christian priorities. It is not an either-or situation. The most important issue is obedience to God.
4. What are some areas other than the political arena in which God may want you to become involved? The media? The arts and entertainment industries? Sports? Law? Science and technology? The educational systems? Do you think secular humanists have taken over these areas, or have Christians abdicated their responsibility to represent Jesus Christ in them?

in PROCESS | *Helping the Homeless*

My husband Gary and I were on our way to a recording session in the Music Row section of Nashville. As we pulled up to one of the busy downtown intersections, a disheveled-looking man stood on the corner, holding out a handwritten sign and a coffee can. His sign read:

> OUT OF WORK
> HOMELESS
> WILL WORK FOR FOOD

If you live or work in any major city in America, you have probably seen similar sights. And if you are like me, your heart breaks a little more every time you see another of these "walking wounded" wandering the streets. Sometimes I want to take my purse and just dump any money I might have into that poor, homeless person's hands.

The plight of the homeless is a major problem in America. Any day or night of the week, regardless of the weather, thousands of men and women (and even children!) can be found living on the streets or beneath highway underpasses, sleeping in cardboard boxes, scrounging through garbage cans, searching for something to eat.

Sure, I know some of the homeless are charlatans. One of the guys who used to beg on a Nashville street corner allegedly garnered over $25,000 per year before he was exposed as a fraud. Other poor people perfect the art of emotional manipulation, tugging at the heartstrings of vulnerable passersby. Moreover, it is no secret that many who beg money for food use the beneficence of well-meaning contributors to buy alcohol or drugs. And yes, some people are penniless and homeless because they are simply lazy and refuse to work, though they are the minority. The circumstances leading to the impoverishment of these people are as varied as the people themselves.

Regardless of the reasons the homeless are on the streets, we are still called to extend our hearts and hands to the needy. But the problem is so enormous. What can we do?

As usual, God was way ahead of us on this one. Take a look at His plan to help the homeless and less fortunate in Deuteronomy 14:28—15:11. Notice especially this verse:

> *There will always be poor people in the land. Therefore I command you to be openhanded toward your brothers and toward the poor and needy in your land (Deuteronomy 15:11, NIV).*

Strange, isn't it? God clearly says that if His people obey Him, they do not have to be poor (15:4, 5). Yet almost in the next "breath," He instructs us to give to our brothers (fellow believers, as well as immediate family members) and to help the needy.

God is a realist. While He has committed Himself to bless His obedient people, He knows that because of sin, some will disobey Him. As a result of greed, selfishness, pride, jealousy, injustice, and other sinful practices, some people will always be poor. Our job is to help them whenever possible, not to conveniently look the other direction.

The question again, though, is how? What can you and I do?

For starters, we can tithe our money by giving God the first ten percent of what we earn. In this passage (14:28, 29), as

God's people were coming out of the wilderness and were about to possess the land He had promised them, the Lord gave them an unusual command. He instructed them to use the entire third year's tithe to support those who were helpless, hungry, or poor. Think about that! What if your pastor announced that every three years, the church will take all the money received in the offering throughout the third year and use it to help support the homeless? Your church board members would probably . . . well, never mind.

Actually, some churches do even better than what God has commanded in this area. Rather than merely giving a full year's income to the poor every three years, they maintain a year-'round benevolent program to help the needy. If your church has such a fund, think and pray about donating some time or money. Many churches have food and clothing banks for the poor. Some take in homeless men and women from the streets and give them a meal and a place to stay for the night. Maybe your church has some other sort of program to help minister to the poor in practical ways. Ask your pastor or youth pastor how you can become involved. If your church doesn't have a program, maybe you can start one.

Certainly you can pray for the spiritual and physical needs of the homeless and the helpless. But be careful; don't use that as an excuse for doing nothing else. Remember, God is a realist. His Word says:

> *If a brother or sister is without clothing and in need of daily food, and one of you says to them, "Go in peace, be warmed and be filled," and yet you do not give them what is necessary for their body, what use is that? Even so faith, if it has no works, is dead, being by itself (James 2:15-17).*

God expects us to use the resources He has given us to help those who are less fortunate.

In process

ZOOM IN

1. How do you feel when you see a homeless person or someone asking for handouts in the street?
2. Next time you see one of our modern-day beggars, remind yourself: *That's somebody's mom or dad; that person is someone's daughter or son.* Or better yet, remind yourself, *There is a person, made in the image of God.* Then ask the Lord how you can best help that individual.

in PROCESS
Hurting People

When Jesus wanted to describe the horrors of hell, He often pointed to a garbage dump outside of Jerusalem, a place called Gehenna. It was a place in which a fire burned constantly in a futile attempt to control the rats, worms, and other vermin that were attracted to the crud. Jesus said that's what hell is like.

I think I've seen it. No, I haven't seen hell or Gehenna, but on a recent trip to Brazil with Compassion International, a Christian relief organization, I believe I saw the world's worst garbage dump.

I thought I had seen most everything when it came to poverty, squalor, and human need. I had taken several trips with Compassion to other impoverished parts of the world, each time thinking, "It can't get any worse than this."

Then I went to Brazil. Our group flew into Rio de Janeiro, one of the most beautiful cities in South America, and also one of the most decadent. Rio is the place most Americans think of when they think of Brazil. You've probably seen pictures of "Christ the Redeemer," the huge statue of Jesus standing with outstretched arms atop Corcovada Mountain, overlooking the tourist hotels of Copacabana Beach. Because the statue is on the highest point around the city, it is one of the first things seen by every planeload of people flying into Rio. It is almost as if Jesus is saying, "Oh, you poor, sinful people. What I could do for you, if you would only come to Me."

in process

On our way into town from the airport, we passed by an area known as "the world's largest slum." More than five hundred thousand people live in tiny one-room shacks that look as though they are stacked one on top of another all over the side of the mountain. Our hosts warned us that it is extremely dangerous to walk through the slum. The area has gotten so bad that even the police refuse to go in there. Drug lords and gangs rule with iron fists and wholesale murders take place every day.

As we drove by the slum, I looked into some of the faces of the common people standing by. I have never before seen such a pathetic sight. The looks on their faces said, "All who enter here abandon hope."

The huge statue of Jesus rose in the distance, a stark, ironic contrast to the sludge of the slum.

We left Rio thinking we had seen the worst of the poverty. We were wrong. We flew up to northern Brazil, to a place called Fortaleza where Compassion has a school for more than nine hundred students. As difficult as it may be for most of us to believe, in Brazil it is considered a tremendous privilege to attend school. Most kids in the country never see the inside of a classroom. The Compassion school is similar to an oasis in a desert. Inside the gates of the school compound, you'd think you were in a typical school in a poor part of the U.S. The students are studying math, history, and all the usual subjects. They can learn to read, write, type, and even participate in intramural sports.

Step outside the school compound, however, and you are in a different world. You are immediately enveloped by the slums. You are in "hell." Filth is everywhere. There are no paved streets, just pressed clay roads. Raw sewage runs freely down the sides of the roads. Pigs, cats, dogs, chickens, and other animals roam freely through the streets foraging for food.

Outside of town is the garbage dump. The dump is so huge, it is virtually impossible to see the end of it, regardless of which way you look. Vultures circle overhead waiting for their opportunity to swoop down and scarf up a free meal. The stench and flies are horrendous. We had to put rags over our mouths to act as makeshift respirators merely to breathe.

But the most appalling part of the dump was the sight of little children, some as young as four or five years old, rummaging through the garbage, searching for something of value that they could sell. Hundreds of men, women, and children climb over the precarious mounds of refuse all day long, looking for glass, metal, or anything else they think the "pawnbrokers" outside the dump might buy. Most of the kids work twelve hours a day, every day, to earn about a dollar. Some of the people of the dump have never known any other life-style.

As I gazed out over the awful sight of the garbage dump, watching young children scramble across the garbage, many of whom were wearing no shoes, it hit me how lost, hopeless, and helpless they are without Christ. I felt compelled to help bring the message of Jesus to those kids . . . somehow, some way.

That's what Compassion International does. Compassion takes the kids out of the dump (with their parents' permission) and gives them a ray of hope through education, as well as an eternal hope through Jesus Christ. Compassion uses the Bible as its lesson book. Bible stories are used in teaching math as well as reading, writing, and history. The entire curriculum is centered around Jesus Christ. As the kids receive an education—their ticket out of the dump—many of them also receive Jesus Christ, their "ticket" out of hell and into heaven.

When I came back home, back to comfortable, affluent America, I tried to express to my friends and family the horrible hold Satan has on the kids of Brazil, and how I felt compelled to help take the Gospel to them. As usual, I was able to say it best in a song, a song I had written before going to Brazil! Now as I sing the words, I understand in a fresh way why the Lord gave me these lyrics:

Little children hurting,
Crying, sometimes dying
By a loved one's hand.
Do you look away,
Maybe shed a tear
But never take a stand?

Ignore your heart and conscience,
Don't see the pain or injustice.

If you love them
won't you show them?
Then we'll help them,
Help the hurting people.
Will you reach out
To their struggles?
Then we'll help them,
Help the hurting people.

(By Kim Boyce/ Julius Drummin; © 1992 Howlin' Hits Music, Inc./ Koreiba Music /Shepherds Fold Music; Used by permission. All rights reserved.)

Take a few minutes and read carefully Matthew 23:1-39. This passage is a scathing rebuke by Jesus to a bunch of people who said they loved God, but their actions said otherwise. Jesus called them hypocrites. Maybe you've never thought of Jesus saying things like this, but He did. As you read, think of that statue of Jesus in Rio, with His arms outstretched to sinful humanity. Notice especially verse 37. In reality, His arms remain outstretched to a sinful world today. But He has asked us, you and me, to be His hands, His feet— to take the message to His children. What are we going to do about it?

ZOOM IN

1. What can you do about the kids in Brazil's dumps? Several things. For starters, you can pray for them. Pray that they find a relationship with Christ. Pray, too, about the possibility of going on a short-term missions trip to Brazil or to some other country, where you can see for yourself the desperate need. Don't worry if you can't speak a foreign language. Neither can I, but everybody in every country understands love when they see and feel it in action.
2. Have you ever seriously prayed about becoming a full-time missionary to a foreign field? The late Keith Green used to sing a song, "Jesus Commands Us to Go," in which he powerfully pointed out that you should assume Jesus has called you to go until He shows you otherwise. Today, perhaps for the first time, ask the Lord if He has something He wants you to do in a foreign land. If He does, He will make a way for you to get there, if you are willing to go.
3. Maybe you are not called into service on a foreign field, but all of us are called to support the work of evangelism at home and around the world. Look for ways you can help fulfill the Great Commission. Then do whatever it is the Lord lays on your heart.
4. If you want more free information about how you can help some hurting people, call Compassion International, toll free: 1-800-336-7676.

in PROCESS

Rx for Boredom

"I'm bored. There's nothing to do around this place."

Sound familiar? Most of us have said that at one time or another in our lives. Furthermore, it's not surprising that kids with time on their hands are often the ones who get into trouble.

But can you imagine ten million bored kids with nothing to do, no purpose, no plans, nothing but time? That's exactly the case in Brazil. Ten million kids literally live on the streets of Brazil's cities. Many of them have been abused physically; some are runaways; most are hooked on drugs. Almost all of them are clueless when it comes to knowing Jesus Christ. Ten million kids! That would be like dumping a city larger than New York or Los Angeles onto the streets.

During my recent trip to Brazil, I saw a girl and her older brother who lived on the streets and made their living by begging and stealing. She was three years old and her "big" brother was five. The sight of those little street urchins nearly ripped my heart out.

The streets of Brazil are crawling with kids at night. One evening during my visit, I went with some Compassion International ministers on a short walking tour, just to get a feel for what these kids' lives are like. I was horrified and exhilarated at the same time. The kids were everywhere, just hanging out, looking for some action. I couldn't help thinking about Jesus' statement:

> *Lift up your eyes, and look on the fields, that they are white for harvest (John 4:35b).*

If you really want to witness for Jesus, there are people all around who need to hear.

We attempted to talk to some of the street kids and finally convinced a group to come back to the Compassion street mission with us. As we were walking back to the mission, one of the kids stole a lady's watch right off her arm! Our Compassion guide chased him down the street, caught him, and made him give the watch back to the woman.

As if that weren't enough excitement, three of the little boys who were walking with us jumped onto the back bumper of a city bus as it sped by. They stuck their feet up under the vehicle and stretched backwards, arms extended, grasping the bumper, and riding with their heads and backs only inches off the ground. I was terrified as I watched them careen through traffic, swinging back and forth with the motion of the bus. Our guide told us that the week before our visit, a little boy had been killed riding a bus bumper. The boy fell off, and the cars behind the bus ran over him.

Another little boy must have gotten bored with our walk, because on a whim he ran right out into the center of a busy street filled with rapidly moving traffic and crouched down—just to see if the cars would stop. Fortunately they did, but one has to wonder how many times he could play that game and live to tell about it.

The kids on those streets were like wild animals—no respect for life, no fear, no rules other than the law of self-preservation. Our hosts told us that every once in a while, the police come through and round up a bunch of the kids, and they are never seen or heard from again. I shudder to think what may happen to them.

Into this barbaric culture, the Lord is calling workers who have a heart for God and a love for kids. Needless to say, this sort of ministry is not for everybody! Frankly, I'm not sure how

In process

long I'd last on the streets of Brazil. But where the Lord calls someone, He gives them the gifts and abilities they need to function in those circumstances. As such, in the heart of the Brazilian ghetto, God is raising a group of witnesses who are reaching out to those kids, one boy or girl at a time.

Ten million kids. Most of them lost and speeding toward hell. Take some time to read Jesus' words in Luke 4:18, 19; then flip over to Paul's insightful message in Romans 10:1-17. Take special note of verses 14 and 15. As you read, ask the Lord to show you what you can do to help reach the kids in Brazil, as well as the kids in your school.

ZOOM IN

1. As a Christian, you have Christ's command and Christ's authority to spread His Gospel. But don't try to do it with your own power. To be effective as a witness, you must allow the Holy Spirit to work through you. Check out Acts 1:8 and you'll see what I mean.
2. A wise man once said, "Witnessing (about Jesus) is just one beggar telling another beggar where to find food!" What do you think he meant by that statement?

in PROCESS
World Changers

Few men and women in history have lived out a radical commitment to Jesus Christ any more dramatically than William and Catherine Booth, founders of the Salvation Army. At the age of thirteen, William yielded his heart to God and committed himself, as much as he knew how, to the service of Christ. Shortly after that, when young Booth heard the dynamic preaching of American evangelist James Caughey, a desire was kindled within William's heart to win men and women to Jesus. But what could a teenager do?

After a long time of prayer and reading the Bible, he hit upon an idea. *I'll simply read the Scriptures to them!* he thought. So William took his Bible and went out to the main thoroughfares of Nottingham, England. There, he stood on a busy street corner and read the Scriptures aloud to any passersby who would take the time to listen. Sometimes, when William felt exceptionally brave, he even ventured to deliver some "off the cuff" remarks concerning the passage he was reading. God was training this young man for his future ministry.

The responses William received were much as you might expect. He was mocked, ridiculed, jeered at, and humiliated by the local gentry of Nottingham. His reading and commentary so infuriated other members of the community that on more than one occasion, bricks were hurled at young Booth in an attempt to silence him. But he refused to give up.

At seventeen, against the wishes of his doctor, William

Booth became a bona fide preacher of the Gospel. One doctor advised him that his health was so poor that he was totally unfit for the strain of the life of a minister. History does not record the physician's sentiments when, fifteen years later, the brash Booth began the organization that is now known as the Salvation Army, a ministry famous for its hearty, open-air street meetings. Today, the Army numbers more than 4 million "soldiers" who work for God in over eighty-six countries.

The "mother" of that huge Army was Catherine Mumford Booth, William's wife and constant co-worker. Converted at the age of sixteen, Catherine Booth knew what it meant to be set apart for God. For this spunky Salvationist, however, separation did not mean isolation. In fact, it was her understanding of Christianity that thrust her into helping solve the most pernicious problems of society. It was because she was set apart for God that she could not sit idly by without trying to change the evils of the world, including homelessness, hunger, alcoholism, and prostitution.

In many ways, Mrs. Booth was far ahead of her time in the area of women's equality and social concern. She often criticized self-centered Christian young women for their laziness and lack of spiritual motivation.

> "It will be a happy day for England," she once observed, "when Christian ladies transfer their attention from poodles and terriers to destitute and starving children." She reminded women that living for pleasure, and filling their days with eating, drinking, dressing, riding and sightseeing, left no time to serve God. They were too occupied with self, she said, to develop spiritual resources.
>
> Edith Dean, *Great Women of the Christian Faith* (New York: Harper & Row, Publishers, 1959; reprinted ed., Westwood, N.J.: Barbour and Company), p. 220.

One of the ways Catherine Booth decided that she could emphasize her separation from the world was through her clothing. Ironically, she was not content to wear ordinary garb which afforded only a barely noticeable differentiation between her appearance and other young women of her time. She wanted the difference to be obvious to even a casual observer. As such, in a day when most intelligent, sophisticated women were piling on the powder and the petticoats, Catherine designed a new look for the women of the Salvation Army—a uniform!

Although the uniform might seem plain by today's standards, it clearly stated to the world that the woman wearing it was on important business and was worthy of respect. Catherine's rationale was simple:

> It seemed clear to me from the teaching of the Bible that Christ's people should be separate from the world in everything which denoted character and that they should not only be separate but appear so. Otherwise what benefit would their separation confer upon others? As I advanced in religious experience I became more and more convinced that my appearance ought to be such as to show everybody with whom I came in contact that I have renounced the pomp and vanities of the world, and that I belonged to Christ. (Ibid., p. 221)

Catherine and William Booth were set apart unto the Lord; they were "clothed in the Holy Spirit," and their lives resulted in effective and fruitful service for Christ. The Booths' influence continues to this day through their writings and through the Salvation Army's positive impact upon society.

In Gary's family and mine, the Salvation Army has had a profound influence. Gary's grandmother, "Nanny Elsie," became a Christian while a young girl as a result of the Salvation Army's efforts. She and "Papa Glenn" continue to be prayer warriors on behalf of the entire family to this day. My dad, too, has served on the local Salvation Army Board of Directors in my hometown of Winter Haven, Florida, for as long as I can remember. Undoubtedly, part of the passion Gary and I have to see lives changed by the power of Christ can be traced back to the fact that William and Catherine Booth allowed themselves to be set apart for God's glory, and became world changers as a result.

How about you? Has your life been set apart for God's glory? Have you allowed the Lord to fill you with His presence and make you into a distinctive witness for Him? Has He given you a fresh sense of divine power and purpose in your life? He will, if you will permit Him to do so. He can do that and much more!

God has called us to be different, to be set apart from the world. That is what the word "holy" implies. To get a better picture of what that means in everyday life, turn to Deuteronomy 7:1-21. This passage was originally given to the people of God by Moses after they had turned away from the Lord and worshiped the golden calf (Exodus 32:1-7). The people had repented and God was giving them another chance. Sound familiar?

ZOOM IN

1. The Booths took their commitment to Christ seriously. It wasn't just a casual thing with them. As a result, they were world changers. What are some steps you can take to begin taking your faith more seriously?
2. Maybe you have been worshiping some false gods lately, the god of pride, the god of popularity, the god of pleasure, or some other false god. If so, you need to do what Israel did: they repented of their sins, and committed themselves afresh to being God's holy people. He has given some out-of-sight promises to those who will allow Him to set them apart from the crowd.
3. How does the passage in Deuteronomy 7:1-21 relate to II Corinthians 6:14—7:1?

in PROCESS

What's Good about the Good News?

have you ever wondered, "If the Gospel is such good news, why don't my friends want to hear it?"

Certainly a society obsessed with sin is never going to embrace purity and holiness. And, yes, Satan seems to be working overtime, attempting to entice your friends and mine, as well as you and me! Evil lurks on every corner: blatant, promiscuous sex on television, occult overtones in a lot of today's music, the New Age movement and satanism in our schools. . . . The list of nasty things surrounding us could go on and on. Okay, so maybe I can't expect my friends to turn cartwheels in excitement when I want to tell them about Jesus.

But maybe—just maybe—our friends don't want to hear the Gospel because we've been giving them the wrong message. They've been hearing us harp on what is wrong with everything in the world. Perhaps it's time we take a cue from the angels who appeared to the shepherds at Jesus' birth, and start "harping" the message:

> *Do not be afraid; for behold, I bring you good news of a great joy which shall be for all the people . . . there has been born for you a Savior, who is Christ the Lord (Luke 2:10, 11).*

Wow! The angel didn't say a word about what a moral mess these guys were; the angel didn't ask about their views on abortion or homosexuality; the angel didn't tell them to join a church or even to purchase a new translation of the Old Testament scrolls. Nope. The angel simply said, "I have great news for you—Jesus is here!"

A lot of your friends and mine tune us out when we start talking about our nation's moral quagmire. Moreover, many of my non-Christian acquaintances aren't all that impressed when I tell them I believe in "traditional family values," as important as you and I know those values are for the survival of our society. Furthermore, most kids I meet in high schools and on college campuses could care less when I try to "enlighten" them and tell of our nation's historic religious roots.

I'm sorry to say it, but the receptivity level nearly drops off the scale when most of us begin discussing such subjects with our non-Christian friends. They look at us as though we are totally irrelevant or totally intolerant, either of which is considered an absolute "no-no" nowadays.

Nevertheless, the one thing almost everyone understands and finds intriguing, if not downright inviting, is the person of Jesus Christ. Not "Jesus" plus our political agenda; not "Jesus" plus our philosophy of life, or anything else; just Jesus—the Person—who He is.

When you think of it, that makes sense. Jesus said:

> *And I, if I be lifted up from the earth, will draw all men to Myself (John 12:32).*

With this statement, Jesus was plainly hinting as to what kind of death He would experience, but His prophetic words have a secondary meaning for us today: Wherever Jesus is lifted up or exalted (as the word is sometimes used in the Bible), He will draw people to Himself!

Isn't that exciting? You don't have to beat your friends over the head with your Bible or convince them you are right. The truth is, if you can talk somebody into becoming a Christian, somebody else can probably talk them out of being a

Christian. But when they see Jesus . . . well, that's a different story.

Jesus instructed us to be "salt and light." Take a look at His plan to attract your friends in Matthew 5:13-16. It's a short passage, but it's really powerful!

Jesus was obviously convinced that we would be much more effective at winning our friends to Him by making them thirsty for living water and allowing His light and love to shine through us, rather than by batting them over the head with a salt block or shining megawatt laser beams in their faces. Have you ever used too much salt on your food? Rather than improving the taste, it ruins it! Similarly, a glowing light illuminates; a glaring light is offensive, and if intense enough, potentially blinding.

On the other hand, if salt has lost its flavor or light is hidden, neither is of any value to anyone. Somewhere in between the two extremes of bowling people over with our message and "wimping out " when it comes to witnessing, is a balanced approach to winning our friends to Christ. Let's spread our "salt" freely, to flavor our world with good works, to make people thirsty for what we have found in our relationship with Jesus, and to be a purifying and preserving element in our society. At the same time let's light up the world with our love—Christ's love, really—shining through us. Maybe then our friends will want to hear the Gospel.

ZOOM IN

1. It's easy to talk about being "salt and light" as long as we keep our conversation theoretical, but what does it really mean in our everyday lives? What is something you can do today to help your friends see Jesus? Be specific.
2. Much of being "salt and light" relates to doing good works, as well as just letting our light shine. Think of something you can do today that will be an unspoken witness for Christ. Then don't say a word about it to anyone (except your heavenly Father); just do it.

in PROCESS *Home Videos*

in PROCESS
Our Incredible Van

Gary and I have a van that just won't quit. We've tried to kill that vehicle in a variety of ways, but like the battery in the commercials, it keeps going and going and . . .

At this writing, the van has more than 150,000 hard miles on it, most of which were traveled while pulling a U-Haul type trailer, loaded down with equipment. For a while we were hoping someone would steal it, but nobody even attempted. Now it's been with us for so long, we're getting sentimental about it. The van is part of our "family."

I purchased the van shortly after I started singing professionally and taking a live band along with me on the road. It was three years old when I bought it, but it had only 17,000 miles on it. I felt the van was the Lord's way of providing transportation for us. Five years later, it's still going! I guess when the Lord gives you the right thing, it works.

On the other hand, if you buy something without the Lord's blessing, it will be a pain in the neck to you no matter how useful, attractive, expensive, or prestigious it may be. Let me give you an example.

Soon after Gary and I married, we wanted to buy a new car. We both had our own cars before marriage, but we wanted one we could call our "family car." We found a beautiful, used BMW at a terrific price, but we weren't sure whether or not we should buy it. It wasn't a question of whether or not the car was worth the money; what troubled us was the stigma that people attach to owning certain types of luxury vehicles. We prayed about buying the car, but we didn't feel we had any absolute answers from the Lord. In retrospect, we know that should have been a hint.

We were, however, getting a lot of encouragement from well-meaning friends.

"Oh, you guys need that car!"

"You can afford it!"

"Everybody who is anybody in the music business is driving a 'Beamer' these days."

"You gotta have that car."

"It's you!"

"As soon as I bought my 'Beamer,' I started getting more business than I could handle."

"It's a classy car, and you're a classy couple. . . . "

And on and on. Our friends' kind remarks played right into the hands of our pride. Before long, we started saying things like, "Well, it really is a great car. And it is too good of a deal to pass by. . . . "

Gary had reservations about the car from the beginning, and I was getting more confused every time we discussed it. Nevertheless, we decided to get the car. We were in Florida at the time, so we called the owner back in Nashville and told him we'd be home in a few days, and we definitely wanted to buy the 'Beamer.' The whole way back, Gary and I had misgivings about the car, but we had given our word. When we got back home, we bought the BMW.

Funny, we had prayed and asked the Lord to give us the car, but now that we had it, we weren't happy with it. The car was great; it was beautiful and had a smooth ride. There was nothing wrong with it. The problem was with us. We really weren't comfortable driving a BMW.

Besides the nagging feeling that we had sort of jumped ahead of the Lord in buying the BMW, I began to feel guilty about driving it, especially after Gary and I went on a trip to Ecuador with Compassion International. Back in the U.S., the inconsistency smacked us right in the face. I mean, there we were trying to raise money to feed, clothe, educate, and evangelize impoverished kids in foreign countries, while at the same time, we were making what we felt were astronomical car payments. Finally, Gary and I said, "Wait a minute! What are we doing driving this car when we could have half the car payment and still have a great car? And we'd still have money left over to give to the Lord's work!"

We knew what we had to do. We decided to sell the car and go back to riding in the van until the Lord opened the doors for us to buy a new car. But we learned several valuable lessons from that BMW.

First, the encouragement of friends, no matter how well-intentioned, is not the voice of God. Job's friends honestly thought they were giving him words of wisdom; they weren't.

Second, if you pray about something and don't have a clear direction from the Lord and peace in your heart about your decision, you better pray again and listen to what God is saying—or not saying. God may be saying, "No," or He may be saying, "Wait." You proceed at your own peril when you decide to plunge ahead by default.

Third, sometimes if you "beat heaven's door down" in your prayers and refuse to hear any answer but the one you want, God may grant your request, but you won't be happy with it. In fact, you may wish you had never been so foolish as to mention the matter. In the Old Testament, a group of God's people had to learn that lesson the hard way. They weren't asking God for BMWs; they were whining to God because of a lack of selections on the menu at the "Wilderness Cafe." Feast your eyes on their story in Numbers 11:4-34.

God's people had been grumbling almost since the day they left Egypt. To listen to them talk, you'd think they were having a picnic there. In reality, they had been living in bondage and working in the slave camps, erecting Pharaoh's buildings and monuments. But God had miraculously delivered them, and He had provided them with food every day for well over a year.

In process

Rather than being amazed at God's supernatural provision in the desert for two million of His people, the Israelites constantly complained about His lack of creativity concerning their diet. "All we ever get to eat is this manna stuff," they groaned. "When are we ever gonna get some meat?"

This time their grumbling was more than Moses could handle. He said, "Why me, Lord? Why'd You ever pick me to have to put up with this moanin', groanin' bunch of ingrates? Where am I gonna get meat for all these people? We're out here in the middle of this desert, and there's not a steakhouse in sight!"

The Lord answered Moses, "Okay, Moses. If they want meat, I'll give them meat." And He did! He rained down enough meat on His people to last for months! He gave them exactly what they asked for; in fact, He gave them so much of what they asked for they got sick of it (11:18-20)! But then, before the people could even enjoy their meal . . .

> *While the meat was still between their teeth, before it was chewed, the anger of the Lord was kindled against the people, and the Lord struck the people with a very severe plague (Numbers 11:33).*

The Lord had answered their prayer; He had given them their request, but it did not bring life. It was the way of death.

Boy, am I glad Gary and I learned our lesson the "easy" way!

ZOOM IN

1. We live in an extremely materialistic society. If we are not careful, it's easy to adopt many of the same attitudes as non-Christians, such as: "Go for the gusto," "grab all you can get," "you only go around once in life," and "the one who dies with the most toys wins." All four of these statements sound good; what could possibly be wrong with them?

2. Have you ever bought something you really didn't need, or couldn't afford, just to "keep up with the Joneses"? Maybe it was a car, or maybe it was a pair of expensive athletic shoes, or some new clothes. Certainly, God wants us to have nice things, doesn't He? When can a nice thing become a bad thing in your life? Think of some warning signs that might alert you to this happening.
3. Today, tell the Lord how much you appreciate His provision for you. Check out the apostle Paul's attitude about material possessions in Philippians 4:11-13.

in PROCESS

Leisurely Days and Lonesome Nights

odern young men and women have more leisure time available, more money to spend, and more opportunities to have fun than any group of young people in history. But if that time is not used constructively, it becomes all too easy to get into trouble.

That's what happened to Dinah, Jacob's daughter. Her story is in Genesis, chapter 34. Take an extra minute today to read the entire chapter. It's only 31 verses, and you won't believe this is in your Bible unless you read it for yourself.

Dinah's story is pretty hot stuff. It's the kind they make soap operas and R-rated movies out of today, but it is, nevertheless, a true account.

You can't blame Dinah for being bored. She was a young woman in her teens who had grown up living out of a suitcase. Her family was constantly on the move, and now that the clan had settled near the city of Shechem, she was anxious to find out what life was like in the big city.

Restless, tired of being alone, and longing for some excitement, Dinah decided to take things into her own hands. She seized the first opportunity to explore Shechem for herself.

"Never a dull moment in Shechem," is what everyone had said. "Shechem shakes night and day!" Dinah had heard about the beautiful city, nestled between the mountains. She had seen some of the fancy, bright-colored clothes that traveling merchants had purchased in the city. Why, Shechem was the cultural and entertainment capital of that part of Canaan! More importantly, Dinah had heard that the girls in Shechem really knew how to have a good time; she assumed that meant the guys were pretty hot numbers too.

Now, as she entered the gates of the city all by herself, she was ready for her wildest dreams to come true. She wasn't looking for trouble. She just wanted to have a little fun.

But trouble took little time to find innocent, naïve Dinah. The prince of the land saw her and was deeply attracted to Dinah, and since he was accustomed to getting everything he wanted, he took her . . . by force. He raped Dinah, the daughter of Jacob.

When Jacob and his boys found out about the defilement of Dinah, they were furious. According to their law, robbing a young woman's virginity was not only a serious crime against her, but it was also an outright insult to the entire family. What complicated things even further was that Jacob and his family had made a covenant with God promising to keep themselves pure and holy, and to refrain from intermarrying among the Canaanite people.

Knowing this, Dinah should have been even more careful to avoid jeopardizing the family name, not just for her own sake; her family was God's witness to the world around them. But Dinah just wanted to have some fun.

Dinah's fun, however, set off a series of reactions—some noble, some nasty. Shechem, the spoiled prince for whom the town was named, proved that he wasn't a total creep. Apparently, he genuinely cared for Dinah, which is more than we would expect of a guy who robs a woman's virginity by raping her. Nevertheless, Shechem seriously desired Dinah to be his wife, and he was willing to pay any price to get her.

When Jacob's sons proposed circumcision as the only circumstance under which they would consent to the marriage, Shechem gulped hard and said, "Okay." The whole city would be circumcised, every man in Shechem, in preparation for the

in process

inevitable intermarrying that would take place once the two families became one.

Shechem and his dad, Hamor, did their part. They had every man in the city circumcised, young and old alike. But Simeon and Levi, two of Jacob's sons, weren't playing this thing straight. They were looking for revenge. They were out for blood. While the men of the city were incapacitated by the pain from their circumcisions, Simeon and Levi took their swords and slaughtered every man in town, including Hamor and Shechem. Then they looted the city, stealing everything in sight—the flocks, the donkeys, the women and children, and anything of value in the peoples' homes.

What had begun as Dinah's innocent pleasure cruise into the city had turned into a debacle of rape, lies, murder, plunder, theft, and kidnapping. Not only had Dinah's name been dragged through the mud, but also that of her father, her brothers, her family, and Shechem's family. Saddest of all, the name of God had been sullied by this whole sordid affair.

Unquestionably, Dinah was scarred for life. Would she ever forget the man who had raped her and then paid for his sin with his life and the lives of an entire city? Would she ever be able to forgive him? Would she ever forgive her brothers, who, in their revenge, took away her only chance to cover her shame by marrying the prince? Would she ever forget that her dad had more concern for maintaining his name than he had for the physical and emotional abuse his daughter had undergone?

No. Dinah would never be the same. Fun, sometimes, just isn't worth it.

ZOOM IN

1. Have you allowed boredom and loneliness to breed problems in your life (overeating, immorality, obsession with "soaps," laziness, or foolish adventurism)?
2. List several creative and constructive ways to spend your free time.

in PROCESS

Switched!

how can it be wrong when it feels so right?

That question is asked about a lot of moral choices, nowadays, and the answer is not always what you think it ought to be, as two friends from New Orleans found out.

James McElveen and his friends, Bernie and Tammy Milligan, were enjoying a summer hike along a lush, central Tennessee mountainside. As they picked their way single file around a slippery ledge next to a waterfall, James placed his foot on what looked to him like a rock, covered with leaves. It wasn't. It was actually the top of a tree that was growing up the side of the slope. James lost his balance and tumbled thirty feet through the foliage, landing facedown and unconscious in eighteen inches of water.

Out of concern for their friend, James's fellow hikers picked him up (not a good idea when someone has a possible back injury), placed him in the backseat of their car, and raced to the nearest hospital, a small community facility ten miles away. James was still unconscious when the hospital orderlies wheeled his gurney into the emergency room.

As a doctor worked on James, a receptionist with a clipboard in her hands approached Bernie Milligan and began asking for some basic information about James—his name, address, and insurance information, that sort of thing. Bernie knew his friend James did not have any health insurance, so without batting an eye, Bernie lied, "His name is Bernie Milligan and he works at

Martin Marietta in New Orleans." Actually it was Bernie who worked as a technician at the Martin Marietta plant, and did have health insurance, but James worked for an entirely different company! Nevertheless, Bernie gave the hospital receptionist his own insurance account number, a compassionate but illegal, fraudulent, and criminal action.

Two days later, James woke up in Nashville's Vanderbilt hospital, where he had been transferred. At first he couldn't remember why he was hospitalized; he just knew that intense pain kept shooting through his back and he was being called Bernie! Before long, however, he realized what his friend had done. As he contemplated what he should do, the doctors informed James that a vertebra had been broken in his back, and surgery was required to remove any possible bone chips which could cause nerve damage. James figured his choices now were to either carry on the facade of being Bernie Milligan or run the risk of being paralyzed. He kept quiet, had the operation, and the hospital and doctors billed Bernie's insurance company.

Back in New Orleans, the lie began to bear heavily upon the real Bernie Milligan's conscience. He was glad that his friend's operation was a success, but Bernie knew that sooner or later the insurance forms were going to show up at Martin Marietta. He went to see a counselor at work, but he couldn't bring himself to confess his wrongdoing. A month later, Bernie was called in by a company insurance investigator to explain his insurance claims for more than $42,000. Bernie tried to play dumb and blamed the bill on a hospital accounting error. His bosses didn't buy it, and Bernie was fired on the spot.

Because Martin Marietta's primary customer was the U.S. Defense Department, the employees were insured by the government. As such, Bernie's fraud was against the U.S. government. Federal agents arrested Bernie and James, as well as Bernie's wife, Tammy. Besides having to pay back every penny of the hospital bills, Bernie was sentenced to nine months in federal prison, James spent seven months in federal prison, and Tammy was sentenced to four months of house arrest.

During their trial, the deceivers discovered that if a hospital receives Medicare and Medicaid funds from the government, federal law demands that emergency care be provided whether a patient has insurance or not. In other words, the doctors would have performed the necessary operation for James anyway! Sure, James would have had to pay the bill out of his own funds, but he would not have been risking paralysis, a jail sentence, or his buddy's job. Their lie cost them much more than the truth would have.

Something similar happened in biblical times when a guy by the name of Jacob thought he could "help God along a bit" by telling some lies. Worse yet, his mom was his partner in crime. To investigate their scam, turn to Genesis 27:1-45.

Jacob meant well in some ways. He had an appreciation for the spiritual benefits bestowed by the family birthright (Genesis 25:19-34) and his father's blessing. His brother, Esau, seemed to care little about either, until it was too late.

As the firstborn son, the birthright and blessing rightfully belonged to Esau. As the oldest son, he was entitled to inherit a double portion of his father's estate. Besides that, the family line, blessed by God, was to continue through him.

But by selling his birthright to Jacob for a bowl of stew, Esau was showing his contempt for God's promises. It was like saying, "Here, God. Here's how little I value Your blessing. I'd rather have a bowl of stew."

Granted, Esau's attitude revealed his lack of respect, but Jacob and his mother, Rebekah, didn't have to deceive Isaac so Jacob could get the blessing intended for Esau. God had spoken to Rebekah while she was still pregnant with Jacob and Esau. The Lord had indicated to her that He was going to provide great things for Jacob and that he would even surpass his brother, Esau. When Jacob and Rebekah conspired to dupe dear old dad, Isaac, they lied; they stole what God had planned to give Jacob in the first place!

Just as the hospital would have taken care of James McElveen without his and Bernie Milligan's deception, God would have

In process

taken care of Jacob without his and Rebekah's treachery. And just as James and Bernie suffered severe consequences for their deception, Jacob and Rebekah paid dearly too.

No, Jacob didn't do time in a federal prison, but he might as well have. At his mother's advice, he ran away and lived with his Uncle Laban in Haran. His actions caused his brother Esau to be extremely angry with him. In fact, Jacob didn't see or speak to his brother Esau again for years, long after they were both married and had children of their own. As for Rebekah, she never saw her beloved son Jacob again. She died before the brothers could be reconciled.

How can it be wrong when it feels so right? No matter how much something may feel right, if it violates God's principles, it's still wrong.

ZOOM IN

1. How would you have handled the situation if you had been in Bernie's place and your best friend had been hospitalized with no insurance? Would you have done the same? What would you have done differently?
2. How do you make those moral and ethical decisions? What is the standard by which you decide right and wrong?
3. The good news is, despite his deception, when Jacob "came clean" with God, the Lord picked him up, brushed him off, and continued to bless him. God gave Jacob the courage to seek reconciliation with his brother, Esau. God changed Jacob's heart, and even changed his name—to Israel. He blessed Israel and made Israel a blessing to the world.

   Despite our deceptions, lies, and other sins, when we seek His forgiveness and commit ourselves to walking in obedience to God, He can still use our lives, bless our lives, and make us blessings to our world.

in PROCESS | *I've Fallen and . . .*

Susan was feeling good, and she was looking good too. A friend had fixed her up for a blind date with the star basketball player from Belmont. Susan had never met Mr. Belmont, but she was one of his most avid secret admirers.

Now, here she was, in the same car with him, making small talk as they motored their way toward the first stop of the church youth-group sponsored progressive dinner. They were scheduled to have soda pop and appetizers here at this first home, after which they would move on to the next house for soup and salad. Then they were to drive across town for the main course, followed by another trek to someone else's home for dessert. It promised to be a wonderfully wild, wacky evening!

Susan and Mr. Belmont arrived slightly late at the first house, so they hurriedly started down the basement steps toward the plush den that had been transformed into a large, formal dining area for the affair. All the other guests were already seated, and every eye was on the stairs as the latecomers started their descent.

Susan was on cloud nineteen. Her elegant evening gown sashayed slightly as she stepped daintily in her high heels down the first step. She had worn her highest heels, hoping to negate some of the distance between Mr. Belmont's height and her own short stature. Those heels, however, were Susan's great undoing.

In process

As she lifted her foot, a fray in the carpet on the steps caught one of the spikes of her heels. Susan tripped, losing her balance on the staircase, and tumbled awkwardly down the steps, violently banging her body as she bounced from step to step. At first, the dinner guests held their breath, until someone discovered that Susan had suffered no physical injuries. Then the snickers turned to outright belly laughs.

Embarrassed and humiliated, Susan attempted to collect her dress and stand to her feet. Unfortunately, in her haste to get out of the stairway and away from the hilarious laughter of her friends, she failed to check her heels. She stood up and immediately toppled over backward again, crashing into a tray table as she fell. The heels had broken off her shoes during her first fall.

All sophistication now gone, Susan lay sprawled helplessly on the floor. Mr. Belmont, who had watched the rise and fall of Susan from atop the stairwell, casually sauntered down the steps, stepped right over Susan with an I-have-no-idea-who-this-woman-is attitude, and took a seat with the other dinner guests.

Stumbling and falling. It happens all the time in the spiritual realm. Sometimes it hurts; other times it is merely frustrating and embarrassing, but it is always a tragedy. And the reaction of your super-pious friends is often the same as Mr. Belmont. "Oh, you're hurting? You've fallen? I really didn't notice," as they step over you, perhaps kicking you again as they go by.

The apostle Paul says Christians should have a different attitude toward their Christian brothers or sisters who fall down or get messed up. Take a minute to check out his words of restoration in Galatians 6:1-10. If you have fallen lately, let these verses be a comfort to you. If you know someone else who has gotten caught in a trespass, let these words be a challenge to you.

An elderly woman reached near-celebrity status in the early 1990s for a single line in a television commercial. "I've fallen," she cried, "and I can't get up!" She was all alone and had nobody to help her. Fortunately, she had purchased an electronic device that enabled her to call for assistance.

If you think about it, that little lady was crying out for all of us. To slip and fall in our attempts to please God is nothing new. Paul reminds us that "all have sinned and fall short of the glory of God" (Romans 3:23). So let's not play any self-righteous, spiritual games. Stumbling is not unusual; maybe it's even to be expected from time to time.

In fact, I'm convinced that God doesn't get nearly so angry when you stumble and fall if you are stumbling in His direction. If you simply call upon Him for help, He will patiently pick you up, brush you off, lovingly discipline you if necessary, and then put you on the right path again. However, if you choose to walk in disobedience, willfully continuing to walk contrary to His direction, you're on your own.

Today, choose to take Paul's advice seriously:

> *Brethren, even if a man is caught in any trespass, you who are spiritual, restore such a one in a spirit of gentleness; each one looking to yourself, lest you too be tempted (Galatians 6:1).*

ZOOM IN

1. In what way have you stumbled recently? Ask God to forgive you and to put you back on your feet.
2. Look for someone who has failed or stumbled; rather than laugh at or talk about the person, encourage him or her.
3. Remember, we've all stumbled in one way or another, and on our own we can't get up. But with Jesus Christ providing the power, and a few friends helping out with encouragement, we can stand again with confidence.

in PROCESS
Trust God and Be Flexible

gary and I were down to the last song on our "Facts of Love" album, after months and months of preparation and work. We had already spent several weeks and thousands of dollars recording all but one song. The day before we were scheduled to go into the studio to begin work on the last song, my manager told us that Todd and Bo Cooper and Vernon Bishop, members of our band, were staying up all night trying to write one final, special song for the album.

We were already scheduled to cut another song, a remake of an old Andrae Crouch song. All the studio musicians had been booked, and Bryan Lenox, our producer for that part of the album, had already written out the studio charts for the session. Gary and I knew the song and how we wanted to do it. Everything was ready, planned out in meticulous detail, just as every other cut on the album had been.

Then we heard the guys' song. It was still untitled and none of the words had been written, but as soon as we heard the music, we knew it was right for the album. Now all we had to do was write the lyrics!

We called Bryan and told him we were going to do a different tune. After he picked himself up from the floor, he said, "You're kidding!"

You may be thinking, *So they changed one song. What's the big deal?* Well, producing an album is a real art, similar to constructing a house. The producer, like the construction foreman, knows exactly what piece goes where on the recording, and which musicians can do the best job in putting it there. For us to swap songs on Bryan the night before going into the studio would be comparable to telling a construction foreman, "Remember those blueprints we have all labored over for months? Well, forget them. Because tomorrow, we're going to begin construction on a totally different house, with no blueprints at all!"

Bryan had scheduled specific studio musicians for the next day's session, because in recording an album, studio musicians are booked for their particular areas of expertise. As great as the Nashville studio players are, not every musician is right for every type of song.

No wonder poor Bryan was in a dither. Still, he agreed that if we felt strongly that the Lord wanted us to go in a different direction, he would figure out the parts for the new song.

Gary and I went over to Todd's house to begin working on the lyrics. I started getting some ideas on the way. Bryan joined us, and we all worked for hours on the lyrics. Later that night, we moved the songwriting session back to our home, where Todd and I finished about sixty percent of the lyrics. Finally, we couldn't go on any longer, and we decided we'd let the rest of the lyrics go until after the session in the morning. The next day, we went into the studio with the song still unfinished. But to our amazement, the studio musicians Bryan had booked played the new song impeccably! We didn't know exactly what the song was going to say, but everyone in the studio sensed it was going to be terrific.

Two days later I was scheduled to sing the lead vocal, and I was still working on the final lyrics when we arrived at the studio. Todd and I fine-tuned the song, and we recorded it. Sure enough, it turned out to be something special. It's called, "Dancin' to the Beat of Your Heart," and to us it is one of the most exciting songs on the album, primarily because of the way it all came together. I think that after months and months of straining to get every detail on the album just right, the Lord wanted to remind us who was in charge!

Take a look at Psalm 127:1, 2. This is a tremendous promise of God, especially for last-minute songwriters! Then turn to Psalm 119:105, 133. Finally, let's look at Proverbs 3:5, 6:

> *Trust in the Lord with all your heart, and do not lean on your own understanding. In all your ways acknowledge Him, and He will make your paths straight.*

ZOOM IN

1. Aren't you glad you have a Master Producer directing your path? Nothing takes Him by surprise; He knows exactly the way the music of your life is to sound. He has promised to guide your steps, and if you will trust Him, He can turn your timid, uncertain notes into "eternal hits"!
2. Sometimes it's a little scary to stay in step with the Lord, because to do so might throw your own plans out of sync. But His way is always best. He's always doing something new and exciting! Sure, you could press all your own buttons on the master control panel of your life, but think of all the great music you would miss.
3. Today, commit yourself to listening for the Master Producer's directions. He will always lead you to His best.

in PROCESS *Until Now*

have you ever heard the classic hymn, "My Jesus, I Love Thee"? The lyrics are so rich and compelling. Remember?

> My Jesus, I love Thee, I know Thou art mine.
> For Thee all the follies of sin I resign;
> My gracious Redeemer, my Saviour art Thou:
> If ever I loved Thee, my Jesus, 'tis now.

A song such as that must have been written by someone who had a wealth of understanding, years of theological training, and probably a lifetime of spiritual experiences upon which to draw. Right?

Nope. The amazing spiritual insights of "My Jesus, I Love Thee" were written by a teenager, William Ralph Featherston of Montreal, about the time the Civil War was being fought in the U.S. The sixteen year old penned the lyrics as an expression of his heartfelt gratitude to Jesus after he found Christ as his Savior. He then sent a copy of his poem to his aunt who lived in Los Angeles. Somehow, the lyrics appeared in an English hymnal, known as *The London Book,* in 1864. The author was said to be "Anonymous."

A few years later, a well-known Baptist preacher, Dr. A. J. Gordon, discovered the lyrics and decided to write another melody for them. The familiar tune of "My Jesus, I Love Thee" was the result of the great preacher's composing. The song has since been included in millions of hymnbooks and has been sung by Christian believers around the world for more than 130 years. Often, this song has been sung in moments of intimate spiritual introspection and deep commitment, as well as times of rededication to the Lord.

Sadly, William Ralph Featherston died in 1873, long before his song became so well known; he was only twenty six years of age. He probably never dreamed of being a songwriter, but the words the teenager wrote continue to inspire millions of people today.

I had never dreamed of being a songwriter, either, but like Featherston, when I began to realize how much Jesus loved me, I couldn't help but express it somehow. Music isn't the only way you can praise and worship the Lord, however. Some people express their love and adoration of Him by writing prose. Others express His creativity by painting, sculpting, performing dramatic works, and yes, even "praise dancing." A group of people at my home church are tremendous blessings to the local body of Christ because they express their gratitude to God by performing puppet shows for children. Whatever gift God has given to you, use it to proclaim your heartfelt feelings to God.

If you aren't sure which method of giving God glory is best for you, explore some possibilities. Try some new ways of expressing your heart. We're all different, so don't worry if what works for somebody else isn't your favorite means of worshiping God.

Putting my thoughts and feelings into music is one of my favorite ways of expressing gratitude for what Christ has done for me. The lyrics of a song on my "Facts of Love" album explain:

Little girls have great big dreams.
Grown-up girls lose hope, it seems.
I don't know why my dreams had to die.

Nobody knew the tears that I cried.
Until now
I know Your love has saved me from the pain.
Until now
Never knew someone like You.
In Your arms Your perfect love brings hope to me again.
Never knew You could make a change somehow.
Until now.

> "Until Now," by Kim Boyce/ Bryan Lenox / B. Cooper; © 1992 Howlin' Hits Music, Inc./ Koreiba Music/ Sunday Shoes Music/ B-B-B Music; Used by permission. All rights reserved.

Take a few moments to read I John 4:7-21 and allow God's incredible, amazing love to wash over you in a fresh way. Memorize I John 4:19 and treasure it in your heart forever.

ZOOM IN

1. Take some time today to express your heartfelt gratitude to Jesus for all He has done for you. If you have trouble putting the words together, try singing "My Jesus, I Love Thee" back to the Lord or feel free to "borrow" my feelings in "Until Now."
2. Maybe God has been prompting you to put some of your thoughts down on paper. Do it. Start today! You don't need to write poetry or lyrics for songs (then again, you may want to!); maybe a diary or a journal is more your style. Whatever works for you, do it. There's something about putting your feelings of love and devotion to Jesus on paper that causes them to come alive in a new and exciting way. Who knows? Maybe a hundred years from now, the world will still be singing your expressions of praise and adoration of the Savior.

in PROCESS

Developing Your Own Pictures

in PROCESS

From Goo, to the Zoo, to You?

I used to think that the three most important ingredients in a person's Christian life were reading the Bible, praying, and going to church. I still believe these disciplines are absolutely essential to a growing Christian life. However, the more I meet and talk with young adults at my concerts, the more convinced I become that the most important factor in the progressive growth of a young Christian is a positive, Christ-centered, biblically based self-image. Without proper self-esteem—that sense of being loved, accepted, and competent—a person may perform the rituals of Christian living, but may end up doing so out of a sense of duty rather than as a result of devotion to the Lord.

Why would anyone not think highly of himself or herself? Why would you not feel that you belong, that you matter, that you can accomplish great things? We all know how important the opinions and comments of our peers and our parents can be as we develop our self-concepts. And what teenager with an older brother or sister hasn't been devastated by an offhand remark from a sibling? Furthermore, we know that our self-image is greatly influenced by what and how we think about ourselves. But there are several sources of low self-esteem you may not have considered.

One cause of poor self-esteem is the fact that we live in an awfully negative world. Have you read the newspapers lately? Listened to the evening newscasts? It's a jungle out there!

Add to that the threat of nuclear annihilation (which has not gone away despite the dissolution of the Soviet Union), the hole in the ozone layer, global warming, world hunger, and a few other humanity-threatening problems facing mankind, and it's pretty easy to get depressed.

Still, a lot has to do with the way we look at it, doesn't it? Exciting, wonderful things happen every day, but we simply don't hear about them. Unfortunately, most positive events are not interesting headline material, as far as the news media are concerned.

Have you ever gone on vacation, and for a few days out of the year, totally ignored radio, TV, and the press? If you have never tried it, next vacation, give it a chance. You'll be amazed how your outlook changes.

Certainly, we need to be knowledgeable about current events. As Christians, we cannot afford to live in isolation. We can, however, limit or balance the amount of negative input we allow into our lives.

Another indirect cause of low self-esteem is that many people have been indoctrinated with Darwin's theory of evolution. If you discount the Genesis account of Creation and accept Mr. Darwin's nebulous theory that you evolved from a blob of goo to a monkey to a human, that in itself is self-deprecating. After all, if you are nothing more than a sophisticated ape, what difference does it make if you waste your life monkeying around?

Have you ever seen the movie "Any Which Way But Loose"? If you haven't, don't bother. I'll fill you in on the entire flick right here: Clint Eastwood meets his match when he encounters an orangutan named Clyde. The movie is funny and Clyde is a brilliant beast, but I'd hate to think of him as my long-lost brother!

Yet, that is precisely the point of Darwinian evolution. No wonder so many teenagers don't know who they are! If you don't know where you came from, you probably won't know why you are here or where you are going, and it will be impossible to become who you were created to be!

Aren't you glad that as Christians, we know that our heavenly Father lovingly designed us as His creations? You are not an accident of evolution. The Creator of the Universe intricately designed you as His crowning achievement! You have been handcrafted by God as a rare treasure. The Bible says:

> *For we are His workmanship, created in Christ Jesus for good works, which God prepared beforehand, that we should walk in them (Ephesians 2:10).*

Before that, however, the Scripture says, "In the beginning God . . ." A wise man once said that if you can believe the first four words of the Bible, you won't have any problem believing the rest of it. Let's check out what he means by reading Genesis 1:1-31. Don't forget to notice the first four words.

ZOOM IN

1. How does the knowledge that God created you affect your daily life? If you say, "It doesn't," how do you think it should?
2. After all these years, Darwin's theory of evolution remains just that—a theory that has never been proven (nor can it be). Why do you think it has received such widespread acceptance in our educational systems?
3. Today, take a moment to thank God for creating a masterpiece—you!
4. Here are a few verses of Scripture that will remind you how special you are to God. I suggest that you memorize these verses and allow the Holy Spirit to use them to continually bolster your self-esteem.

> *I praise you because I am fearfully and wonderfully made;*

>   your works are wonderful,
>   I know that full well.
>   My frame was not hidden from you
>   when I was made in the secret place.
>   When I was woven together in the
>   depths of the earth,
>   your eyes saw my unformed body.
>   All the days ordained for me
>   were written in your book
>   before one of them came to be.
>   Psalm 139:14-16 (NIV)

Then God said, "Let Us make man in Our image, according to Our likeness." . . . And God created man in His own image, in the image of God He created him; male and female He created them.
Genesis 1:26, 27

. . . you were not redeemed with perishable things like silver or gold . . . but with precious blood, as of a lamb unblemished and spotless, the blood of Christ.
I Peter 1:18, 19

For the Lord will be your confidence,
And will keep your foot from being caught.
Proverbs 3:26

For as he thinks within himself, so he is.
Proverbs 23:7a

This is love: not that we loved God, but that he loved us and sent his Son as an atoning sacrifice for our sins.
I John 4:10 (NIV)

These things I have spoken to you, that My joy may be in you, and that your joy may be made full.
John 15:11

in PROCESS

What You See Is What You Get

bob Moawad, a motivational speaker who does most of his work in high schools, tells a bizarre but true story about a man who somehow got himself locked in a railroad refrigerator car. With the door shut tightly and no apparent escape, he sat down to await his inevitable death by freezing or suffocation, whichever came first.

To pass the time, he decided to chronicle his demise by writing his thoughts on the wall of the railroad car. His first statement was: "It's getting colder in here." Later he wrote, "I'm freezing to death!" A few hours later he scribbled, "Nothing to do. Nothing to do but wait. . . ." Several hours later, he wrote, "These may be my last words . . ." and they were. He died.

When the door was finally opened, the rescuers found him dead, but the temperature of the car was fifty-six degrees Fahrenheit! The refrigeration unit on the car had been out of order for some time and was not functioning at the time of the man's death. He died, apparently, because he saw himself as doomed, with no way out.

For that man, the old adage, "Life is a self-fulfilling prophecy," held true. What he feared or expected to happen, came to pass. It usually will in your life, as well. Remember: How you "see" yourself determines how you perform and what you can expect to receive in life.

The Bible makes it clear that your attitudes and thoughts have an overwhelming influence upon the way you do things.

> *For as he thinks within himself, so he is (Proverbs 23:7a).*

Modern psychologists have verified this biblical principle in everyday life. They have discovered that human beings move—consciously or unconsciously—toward that which their thoughts dwell upon, whether victory or defeat, success or failure.

Perhaps that's another reason the apostle Paul instructed us to think positively rather than negatively. Paul said:

> *. . . whatever is true, whatever is honorable, whatever is right, whatever is pure, whatever is lovely, whatever is of good repute, if there is any excellence and if anything worthy of praise, let your mind dwell on these things (Philippians 4:8).*

To help build your faith in the Lord and confidence in yourself, it really helps to think of God's promises to you (there are hundreds of them in the Bible), and to remind yourself of answered prayers. Reflect on the positive instances where you put your faith on the line, and God answered in a specific way. Remember how God has guided you, how He has blessed you in the past, and He will give you tremendous confidence to face a current, difficult situation.

For example, the next time you are assigned to make a speech in class, flip back through the images of all the successful speeches you have made. Don't dwell on the one time the teacher called your name, and in your attempt to get out of your chair, you ripped out the back of your jeans! Don't dwell on the funny speech you thought you made, only to discover afterwards that your zipper had been down throughout your performance!

If you want to increase your confidence, scan back through some great speeches you have made. If you haven't made any yet, then make one now. Make your speech to Mom and Dad, maybe your baby brother, or if nobody else will listen, make your speech to the mirror! Then when it's time for the real thing, concentrate on how well you have done in the past. That will give you confidence for the present and faith to draw upon in the future.

In the same way, next time you want to ask that special someone to the class party, flip back to all the times your invitations have been accepted, not the one time you were told to drop dead!

When you want to share your faith in Christ with a friend, think back to the many times your witness has been positively received. If you've never had such an experience, then think of how you would like such an encounter to turn out. Think about sharing your testimony, or what it means to be a Christian, with another person, and having that person respond by wanting to know how he or she can meet Jesus.

Ask the Lord to help you get the picture that He has of you and know what He wants you to become. He wants much more for you than mere worldly success; He wants you to find true riches that will never fade away (Revelation 3:17-22). Get His painting of you in mind, and keep it always before you. Then start moving toward it, one step at a time.

ZOOM IN

1. Today, read and memorize Philippians 4:13. This is one of the most powerful affirmations a Christian can make. What are some things you want to do that will require you to trust Christ for special strength?
2. Just for fun, first thing tomorrow morning, jot down a brief description of how you think your day will be. Then tomorrow evening, jot down what actually occurred. How do the two lists compare?
3. Read Matthew 9:29 and Matthew 17:20. How do these verses relate to your faith and what you feel God wants you to do and be?

in PROCESS

The Dream Robber

Satan is a thief, and he would love to steal your dreams! No, I'm not talking about nightmares or daydreams. The devil would be happy to fill your head with those! I am referring, however, to the bold dreams the Holy Spirit gives us, the visions He wants us to have and wants to see fulfilled in our lives.

One of the world's most successful soap salesmen is a fellow by the name of Dexter Yager. Actually, Dexter has sold extensively more than just soap to earn his fortune. Still, the product Dexter sells best is Dexter! With his positive self-image, Dexter Yager has become proficient at "selling himself" as a person. One of his favorite challenges to audiences who would aspire to walk in his footsteps is, "Don't let anyone steal your dream!" In other words, be careful about associating with or adopting the attitudes of other people who, through their negative outlook and lack of self-esteem, will rob you of the greatness God has planned for you.

A classic illustration of "attempted dream robbing" took place when the people of God, who had been delivered from the devil's bondage in Egypt, came to the borders of Canaan, God's dreamland for them. Take a peek at their story in Numbers 13:1, 2 and Numbers 13:17—14:12.

God had promised His people a rich possession, a land flowing with milk and honey, a fantastic future! There was only one problem: The place the Lord had created for His people was already inhabited!

Knowing that they might be in for a fight, Moses sent twelve spies into Canaan to check out the opposition. After forty days, the scouts came back with their report.

"It's just like we heard!" they excitedly shared with the welcome party.

And all the people said, "Amen."

"It is a land flowing with milk and honey," the spies continued. "Look at these grapes! Look at these pomegranates! Why, they're the biggest and best tasting we've ever seen! And, here! Taste some of this honey. Isn't that something else?"

And all the people said, "Amen."

Then came the bad news. "But, there are giants in the land, and compared to them, we look like a bunch of grasshoppers!"

And all the people said, "Oh me, oh my!"

"Therefore," concluded the spies, "we are not able to go in and take the land."

And all the people said, "We hear ya, spies! Let's go back to Egypt!"

All the people except two, that is (possibly four, if we count Moses and Aaron). Joshua and Caleb, two of the scouts, said, "Whoa! Not so! We are well able to possess the land, because our God has given it to us!"

Joshua and Caleb were not naïve, optimistic, positive thinkers. They had the same facts as their fellow spies. They admitted the existence of the giants, the opposition, the obstacles. But the difference was in their attitude. They believed God! Their self-images were such that they refused to see themselves as grasshoppers ready to be stomped upon. Instead they saw themselves as God's men. Joshua and Caleb had the same data as the doubters, but they drew different conclusions because they trusted God's promises to them, and they would not allow anyone else to steal their dreams!

Consequently, of approximately two million people who came out of Egypt, only two—Joshua and Caleb—eventually entered God's promised land. The others were a reproach to God's name. They dishonored Him, and as a result, they spent the rest of their lives wandering around in circles throughout the wilderness, until they finally died. Due to their lack of self-esteem, they had allowed the devil to defeat and rob them of God's great dream for their future.

How is your dream? Is it still intact? If your dream has been damaged, delayed, or destroyed, it may be because the devil has deceived you into seeing yourself as a grasshopper. And we know that how we see ourselves is how we will perform. Don't let Satan steal your dream! Don't underestimate what the Lord wants to do in, through, and for you!

ZOOM IN

1. Can you think of a time when Satan robbed you through low self-esteem? What can you do to build it back up when he has? How can you prevent the same thing from happening in the future?
2. What are some dreams you feel God has given you? Are there steps you can take today that will help those dreams come true? If so, list several and keep them someplace where you can review them once a week.

in PROCESS

Guarding Your Dreams

"that guy makes me so mad, I could deck him!" Craig roared, as he slammed his books on the cafeteria table.

"What guy?" his steady girlfriend, Melody, asked.

"Coach Stevens. That's what guy. He passed over me again for the quarterback position on the football team. In place of me, he picked Nate Williams, the guy I have been working out with all summer long. Coach seems to be doing everything he can to keep me from playing that position."

"Why would he do that?"

"I don't know. I think he's trying to make me mad enough to quit. He knew I wanted that position. I've worked hard for it. I've memorized our playbook. I've earned a shot at quarterback. But I'm never going to get a chance to prove myself as long as Coach Stevens is in my way."

"Or as long as you have that chip on your shoulder," Melody answered with a slight smile.

"Oh, yeah; listen to 'Little Miss Self-Righteous' here. Let me polish your halo."

"Okay," Melody shrugged as she spoke, "have it your way. But I'm telling you the truth."

"Yeah, I guess you're right," Craig replied as he slumped into a chair at the table. "But playing quarterback has always been my dream. How am I supposed to go back out there when the coach keeps blasting me? And why should I work so hard just so someone else can use me as a stepping-stone? I don't think I want to play that game anymore."

What can you do when your dreams have been pulled out from under you, when you realize that the things you had always hoped for just aren't going to happen?

For a couple of clues, sneak a peek at a snapshot of Joseph's life in Genesis 39:20—40:23.

Joseph was in prison, incarcerated on an unjust charge, but God hadn't forgotten him. In fact, the Scripture says:

> *The Lord was with Joseph and extended kindness to him, and gave him favor in the sight of the chief jailer (Genesis 39:21).*

Before long, Joseph was running the prison for the jailer! The Bible says:

> *... whatever he did, the Lord made to prosper (Genesis 39:23).*

And Joseph remained faithful to the Lord, even when he was down in the pits!

Joseph refused to become bitter. He also rejected the natural temptation toward self-pity. Perhaps, equally important, he didn't waste his time (and he had several years of his life to waste, if he had wanted to do so) assessing blame upon anybody else who had played a part in his imprisonment. Remarkably, he remained sensitive to the needs of others and allowed God to work through him in those awful circumstances. For example, Pharaoh's cupbearer and baker had been thrown into the same prison as Joseph, and one night, both men had disturbing dreams. Now check this out:

> *When Joseph came to them in the morning and observed them, behold, they were dejected. And he asked ... "Why are your faces so sad today?" (Genesis 40:6, 7).*

Can you believe this guy? What an attitude! His God-given dream had been detoured several times through the dastardly deeds of other people, yet he was still concerned about these guys. Maybe the greatest miracle was not that Joseph was later able to interpret their dreams, but that he noticed the dejection in their faces in the first place. Joseph was committed to being a person God could use, regardless of the circumstances.

In your life, when things don't work out as you had planned, challenge yourself to be a Joseph. Guard against bitterness, self-pity, or blame, and take definite action to use your present circumstances for God's glory.

Bitterness blinds your vision. Resentment and revenge for something somebody said or did in the past will only rob you of your joy today and ruin God's plan for your future. Furthermore, it is impossible to maintain a right relationship with God when you willfully tolerate bitterness in your heart.

Self-pity and blame are also sure roads to alienation and self-destruction. Self-pity is nothing less than disenchanted egotism. It is pride turned upside down. You know how it goes: "Poor, poor, pitiful me. I didn't get what I wanted so I guess I'll eat some dirt!"

When you blame other people for your troubles, you alienate yourself. You become bitter, resentful, and filled with a strange poisonous venom that stings the other person and always destroys a part of you in the process. Similarly, if you blame yourself for your soured dreams, you snuff out your passion and goals and lower your self-worth. If you blame God for your disappointments, you cut yourself off from the one person who can truly help you through your tough times.

Weird, isn't it? No matter who you blame for dashing your dreams, you get worse rather than better.

I tasted some of that cup of bitterness when I participated in the Miss America Pageant, representing my home state as Miss Florida. I hadn't grown up dreaming of being Miss America. Sure, I had thoughts of how great it might be . . . for a few minutes. But I can't say I was obsessed with winning, not even when I was selected as one of the top ten finalists.

In process

Still, when the master of ceremonies, Gary Collins, announced on national television that the 1984 Miss America was Vanessa Williams, something died inside of me. I didn't realize it at the time, but later, much later, after I was far away from the bright lights of Atlantic City and back home in Florida, the realization began to hit me: "I will never be Miss America. That's one dream that will never come true."

Yet at the same time I had a strong sense that God was with me and He was going to do something even better in my life than allow me to be Miss America. And He has!

It's important that we never give up, that we commit ourselves to use whatever circumstances we're in for Christ's honor and glory, and that we keep believing God for His best in our lives. The old saying is true: "When God closes the door, He opens up a window." Loren Cunningham, president of Youth with a Mission, puts it this way: "God delights in taking lemons and making them into lemonade!"

ZOOM IN

1. Have you ever had one of your dreams delayed, detoured, or even destroyed? How did you handle it? Why do you think God allowed it to happen? With Joseph as your example, what could you do differently if you are ever confronted with a similar situation?
2. It's not always easy to trust that the Lord causes

   . . . all things to work together for good to those who love God, to those who are called according to His purpose (Romans 8:28).

   All things include the sins, mistakes, and evil intentions of other individuals who have negatively influenced your life. Today, tell the Lord that you are going to trust Him, no matter how dark the circumstances, and then ask Him to use you to point people to His light.

in PROCESS

Getting Where You Are Going

gary and I have always been goal setters—in our individual lives, in our ministry, in our music careers, and now, in our marriage. Even before I met Gary though, I had learned the value of setting realistic milestones and going for them.

When I came to Nashville to begin working in music, one of the first things my manager did was to sit down with me and make me write out the goals I had for my career and ministry. It was awkward at first, because he encouraged me to be specific about where I saw myself in one year, five years, ten years down the road, and how I planned to get there. I had some great big dreams that I felt the Lord had given to me, but to actually write them down on paper seemed almost a bit presumptuous.

Looking back, I now see that setting those goals early in my music career was one of the best things I ever did. What is really astounding now is to read some of the goals I had written down a long time ago, almost as a wish list of what I hoped God would be able to do with me, and to see how the Lord has brought them to pass. Don't get me wrong. I'm not saying that all I had to do was make a list and keep it under my pillow, and God granted all those requests. But I am saying that by setting my sails in what I believed was a God-given direction for my life, I have been able to chart my course, rather than be controlled by the whims of the water and the wind.

Some people say they don't like to set goals because it puts too much pressure on them. By not setting goals, however, they are literally abdicating the responsibility of their lives, giving it over to chance. As the saying goes, by failing to plan, they plan to fail! Or, as one wise wag quipped, "If you don't care where you're headin', it doesn't matter which road you take."

What about Christians? Should we meticulously draw up our plans and goals, or should we simply sit back with a fatalistic trust, hoping that everything will work out okay? Although it may seem absurd to you, some Christians are especially adept at spiritualizing their lack of goal setting and planning.

"Well, I'll just trust the Lord, and leave the planning up to Him," we often hear.

"God is in charge of my life, and if He wants me to get a college education, He'll be sure to let me know!"

A lot of Christians are reluctant to set goals because they are afraid of what it will look like if they fail. As for Gary and me, we'd rather attempt something great for God and fail, than attempt to do nothing and succeed!

Certainly, our trust must be in Jesus Christ, not simply in our own wisdom, abilities, plans, gimmicks, or success formulas. God is committed to doing His one hundred percent, but He also expects us to use all the sanctified sense He gave us to do our one hundred percent. Part of that entails planning, setting goals, and having a clear vision for the future.

If your goals are intended for evil or if your plans are selfish in nature, you cannot expect the blessing and help of the Lord. He is more interested in your motivation than your success.

> *All the ways of a man are clean in his own sight,*
> *But the Lord weighs the motives (Proverbs 16:2).*

On the other hand, if your goals are godly and good, you can proceed with confidence.

> *Commit your works to the Lord,*
> *And your plans will be established (Proverbs 16:3).*

Set your sights, plan your goals, but always remember:

*The mind of man plans his way,
But the Lord directs his steps (Proverbs 16:9).*

In other words, you may make the plans, but it takes God to make them come about.

The experience of Joseph is a good example of a guy with some lofty, God-given goals. Make it a goal today to read an exciting portion of his story found in Genesis 41:14-57.

Acting upon the revelation he had received from God that a famine was coming to the land of Egypt, Joseph advised Pharaoh to tax the people twenty percent of the land's produce. This food, Joseph said, should be stored up for use during the tough times to come. Pharaoh thought it was such a splendid plan, he put Joseph in charge of overseeing its operation.

Most likely, many of Joseph's peers thought his planning was foolish and unnecessary. "Hey, Joe! What's the big idea? Why not live and let live? Relax. Take it easy! There's plenty of food. These are great days! Let's party! Eat, drink, and be merry, for tomorrow we may die!"

When the famine came, however, they were unprepared victims. They had failed to plan. But Joseph was unwilling to leave his future up to chance. He said, "This is the direction we are heading, here's how we're going to do it, and this is what we expect to happen." He combined his knowledge of the Word of God with good common sense; he saw what needed to be done, and he initiated a plan of action designed to bring it to pass.

The apostle Paul was another planner. He was goal-oriented; he was not a wandering generality, looking for something to do with his life. He said:

I press on toward the goal for the prize of the upward call of God in Christ Jesus (Philippians 3:14).

Paul was not the kind of guy who was content shuffling papers, trifling in trivia, majoring in minors, or indulging in mindless, tension-relieving activities. Can you imagine the great apostle sitting at home every afternoon, watching soaps or situation comedies?

On the contrary, he was a fierce competitor in the ultimate, all-or-nothing battle—the fight for the eternal souls of men and women. He could hardly believe that a Christian would allow himself or herself to run a haphazard course for Christ. To the Corinthians he wrote:

> *Do you not know that those who run in a race all run, but only one receives the prize? Run in such a way that you may win (I Corinthians 9:24).*

Paul was never so headstrong about his own plans, however, that he neglected the leading of the Holy Spirit. Once when he had planned to go into a place called Bithynia, the Spirit of Jesus did not permit him (Acts 16:6-10). Instead, the Lord led Paul to go into Macedonia. The apostle changed his plans to coincide with the Lord's leading, and as a result, exciting new doors of opportunity opened in Paul's ministry.

Goal setting and planning also made sense to Jesus. When He was teaching about the exacting costs of discipleship, He asked the searching question:

> *For which one of you, when he wants to build a tower, does not first sit down and calculate the cost, to see if he has enough to complete it? Otherwise, when he has laid a foundation, and is not able to finish, all who observe it begin to ridicule him, saying, "This man began to build and was not able to finish" (Luke 14:28-30).*

In His own life, Jesus was constantly aware of the Father's plan. He knew His life was not an accident. Consequently He lived His life on purpose. He knew where He had come from, what He was doing here, and where He was going. The night before the crucifixion, Jesus explained to His disciples:

> *I came forth from the Father, and have come into the world; I am leaving the world again, and going to the Father (John 16:28).*

Because Jesus had His goal ever before Him, He would not be distracted or detoured, not by the clamoring masses, not even by His best friends.

ZOOM IN

1. What are goals? A goal is a purpose, an aim, a plan; it is something that, with the Lord's assistance, you work toward. It is a statement of your faith, an expression of your belief in yourself and in God. It is like saying, "God, to the best of my knowledge and awareness, this is what I think You want me to do and how I believe You want me to go about it. If I'm out of line, please show me. If I'm on target, please bless my best efforts."
2. Begin setting some goals of your own today. Pray about what the Lord wants you to do, the direction He wants you to go, and then begin to spell it out on paper. Write down, as specifically and in as much detail as you can, some of your immediate goals—where you would like to be six months from now, a year from now, five years from now. If you are really bold, go ahead and write out how you see yourself and what you believe you will be doing twenty years from now, if the Lord wills.
3. Talk with your parents, pastor, or youth pastor about your goals. Begin to think and pray as specifically as possible about what it is you feel the Lord wants you to do, and what tangible steps you must take to bring it to pass. Remember: He will do His part as you are faithful to do yours.

in PROCESS
You Can Do It!

I will always be grateful to my parents for helping me develop a positive self-image. Mom and Dad were extremely aware of the impression words can make on a young person's mind. As such, Dad would not allow my sisters and me to ever call each other names, not even in fun. He would not tolerate us saying negative things such as:

"You klutz!"

"You dummy! You can't do anything right, can you?"

"Everything I touch, I mess up."

"I guess I'm no good for anything."

Or the worst comment of all: "God could never use somebody like me."

Mom and Dad taught my sisters and me to trust totally in God, and to have confidence in ourselves. It wasn't a pride thing. It was knowing who we were as children of God. I have no doubt that because Mom and Dad were so careful to guard and encourage our self-esteem as we were growing up, I am now able to stand on stage in front of thousands of people and sing about what the Lord means to me.

Sadly, I meet many young men and women whose low self-esteem sabotages their Christian service. They don't believe they can make a difference in the world, so they don't. They don't believe they can be used of God, so they usually aren't.

Mother Teresa, the Nobel prize winner who worked for years among the street people of Calcutta, had a pet saying: Do "something beautiful for God." Yet how many times have you missed out on opportunities to do just that, because of your low self-esteem?

"Oh, I could never sing in the choir! I can't carry a tune in a bucket!"

"Be a part of an evangelistic visitation team? Why, I'd be scared to death! What if we were visiting in a home and somebody asked me to defend my faith? What would I do then?"

"What? Me teach a Sunday school class? Ho, boy! You've got the wrong person. I'd ruin that class!"

Do you hear it from others? Do you hear it coming out of your own mouth? Self-deprecation! You're telling God and yourself what you can't do, rather than what you can do!

Now, obviously, not every one of us is gifted in every area. I have some friends who I prefer not to hear sing; at least, not unless they can be mixed back in the crowd . . . I mean way back in the crowd. Not all of us are talented as teachers or witness leaders. But why concentrate on what we can't do, or don't do well? God has given each of us certain spiritual gifts (Romans 12:3-8; I Corinthians 12:4-31, and Ephesians 4:11-12) to be used for His glory as we build up His church and help others in the world. It's what you do with what you have that matters most to God. All of us can do "something beautiful for God."

Ability and talent are not prerequisites to service in Christ's kingdom. What it really takes is a dedication to Him, and a realization that He can use your life to touch others. Look at the people God has used down through history. Most of them were pretty unspectacular on their own. But they believed in God! And they believed in themselves, in that they were willing to allow Him to use what little bit they had.

I've always been enamored with the little boy who figured so largely in the feeding of the five thousand, as recorded in John 6:1-14. Take a few moments right now to read that account again and then come back here and let's look at it more closely.

Did you notice that everything Jesus used to perform this huge miracle was really quite small in itself? It was a little boy who brought five little loaves of bread, and two little fish to Jesus. Middle Eastern bread is flat, almost like two pancakes stuck together; not at all like the large loaves with which we are accustomed. The fish were small, sardine-like fish; not eighteen-inch rainbow trout like the ones you missed in the mountains!

Yet this little boy, with his little loaves and his little fish, had a little bit of faith! When he presented what little he had to Jesus, the Lord took it, blessed it, broke it, and was able to supernaturally minister to the needs of thousands that day! All because a little boy gave what little bit he had to the Master.

This is more than merely a cute Bible story; the little boy's actions and attitudes are a pattern God gives to us and expects us to emulate. A guy by the name of George Müller understood this example quite well.

As a young man, George wanted to do "something beautiful for God." He had a desire to help the street orphans in England. Though his desire was great, George's wallet was empty. He had only the equivalent of about fifty cents, and he felt that God wanted him to give away even that! Obediently, George gave the fifty cents. And God gave him back fifty cents more.

Right there, George Müller learned a valuable lesson that many of us only talk about: "You can't out-give God!" George continued to give to God and to pray for the Lord's provision. And God refused to let His man down. George Müller sent out no letters asking for money. In fact, he made a point of never revealing his need of financial assistance to any human being. George depended upon God to supply what was required to do His work. Consequently, the Lord used George Müller to begin a ministry with just a few orphans in a rented house in Bristol, England, which soon blossomed into a huge complex of buildings, housing more than two thousand children! Before George turned the orphanages over to someone else, late in his life, God had blessed him with more than two million dollars to use for His glory. And George used every penny of it to help other orphans.

Though George Müller was an eminently humble man, and had a strong sense of his own sinfulness, he would not allow Satan to deceive him into believing that he was useless in God's kingdom. Instead, he threw himself upon the mercy of the Lord, and then threw himself into the magnificent mission of God.

Don't allow Satan to sabotage your Christian service by sinking your self-esteem! Don't allow him to ruin your relationships, destroy your dreams, or paralyze your potential. Rise up, and do something beautiful for God!

ZOOM IN

1. Think back on opportunities to serve the Lord you may have missed because of a poor self-image. How could you have taken advantage of those opportunities had your self-esteem been higher?
2. George Müller was a man of faith. His life story would be well worth your time reading. (There are several books available on his life, including *George Müller of Bristol,* by Arthur T. Pierson. Ask your pastor or check with your church librarian for others.)
3. What do you want to do that you know can only be completed with God's supernatural assistance? Pray about that goal right now and commit it to the Lord.

in PROCESS
Complete Exposure

have you ever watched a photographer working in a darkroom? Pretty wild, isn't it? To someone unfamiliar with the developing process, it all looks strange, mysterious, and almost weird. The room is illuminated by an ethereal red light that casts an unusual pall over the place. The photographer's work bench is lined with trays filled with developing solutions, and the area above the developing trays is usually cluttered with an assortment of already developed photographs that have been hung up to dry. As you look around, you fret, *Maybe I should have taken my film to a one-hour photo processing place!*

The developer knows, however, that great photographs cannot be rushed. Each step of the process is somewhat messy and requires special attention. The latent images in your camera must first be made into negatives. Then the negatives are used to produce the prints. The process involves the careful application of just the right amounts of chemical solutions:

- alkaline and acidic rinses, which turn the images on your film into actual pictures the world can see;
- fixing solutions, which cause your photo images to stabilize and remain intact on the paper;
- washing solutions, which thoroughly cleanse the paper and prevent water spots and streaks on your finished photos.

If any part of the developing process is ignored, forgotten, or circumvented, the quality of your photo is jeopardized. Regardless of the fantastic images on your film, if you don't allow time for proper development, you could easily end up with a blank roll of film, good for nothing but pitching into the garbage.

In many ways, our lives are similar to photographs. Just as a photograph is a reproduction and a reminder of the original experience, our lives are "reproductions" and reminders of Jesus. We are called not only to experience Christ for ourselves, but also to "re-present" Him to everyone who views our lives. A photograph requires proper development if it is going to be a quality reproduction of the original; so do your life and mine.

That's why I am so excited about the stories you have just read. Through them, I believe God is developing you into something beautiful. Please don't try to rush the process. The "Master Developer" is at work in you, equipping you:

> *. . . in every good thing to do His will, working in us that which is pleasing in His sight, through Jesus Christ, to whom be the glory forever and ever. Amen (Hebrews 13:21).*

What an incredible message: God Himself is developing us into His image!

God is taking the raw film of our lives and turning the negatives into positive prints—His prints—intended to reflect His marvelous glory. Granted, sometimes the "alkaline rinse" stings as He exposes hidden images and brings them to the surface in our lives. At times the "acidic rinse" causes us to cringe and squirm in discomfort and doubt as God strips away the impurities that might blur the reflection of His image in us. But through it all, He is carefully conducting the process. He is developing us, washing us with the water of His Word:

> *that He might present to Himself the church in all her glory, having no spot or wrinkle or any such thing; but that she should be holy and blameless"* (Ephesians 5:27).

The result is a fabulous picture of Jesus Christ in us, the hope of glory (Colossians 1:27).

Wherever you are "in process" with the Lord, keep in mind two important principles. First, God has you there on purpose. He wants to teach you some things about Himself, yourself, or the world in which He wants you to represent Him. He hasn't forgotten you; you haven't escaped His notice. God never has to say, "Oh, golly, gee! I forgot about Shelly soaking over there in the alkaline," or "Oops! I guess I used too much acid on poor Steve." No, the Master Developer knows exactly what you need, and He is working to bring out the best in you.

Second, always remember that this life is a process. We haven't arrived yet. None of us can say, "See, look at me! I am a perfect, finished photograph." On the contrary, God is always taking us back to the darkroom for another dip, cleansing us of accumulated crud, bringing out highlights, adding depth and color to our lives. This refining process won't end until we see Jesus face to face. In the meantime, let's make the apostle Paul's words our prayer:

> *That I may know Him, and the power of His resurrection and the fellowship of His sufferings, being conformed to His death; in order that I may attain to the resurrection from the dead.*
>
> *Not that I have already obtained it, or have already become perfect, but I press on in order that I may lay hold of that for which also I was laid hold of by Christ Jesus.*
>
> *Brethren, I do not regard myself as having laid hold of it yet; but one thing I do: forgetting what*

lies behind and reaching forward to what lies ahead, I press on toward the goal for the prize of the upward call of God in Christ Jesus.
Philippians 3:10-14

Now that's a process we don't want to miss!